Date Due

With the Indians of the Pacific

With the Indians of the Pacific

NURSE B. J. BANFILL

THE RYERSON PRESS

TORONTO - CANADA

First published in Canada in 1966 by
THE RYERSON PRESS
299 Queen Street West, Toronto 2B, Ontario

© *William Kimber & Co. Limited 1966*

Made and printed in Great Britain by Tonbridge Printers Ltd
Peach Hall Works, Tonbridge, Kent

Contents

Author's Note

In this book I have tried to describe how I came to appreciate the Indian way of life in the time I was working among them; the incidents are all drawn from my own experience, though I have thought it proper to give fictitious names to the people, places and reservations concerned.

With the Indians of the Pacific

CHAPTER 1

EN ROUTE FOR TOKAWAKA

I stood on Victoria wharf, British Columbia, with Ellen Morris and John Bell, the school teachers, with whom I would work, and who were to become my intimate friends, and I sniffed the delicious, exhilarating sea ozone, and a pleasant nostalgia for the sea and its fishermen swept over me. I wondered if I had Indian blood in my veins.

Curiosity had compelled me to learn about Indians at first-hand. I knew the word 'Indian'. I had seen Indians, but knew little about these first North American citizens. But until now, remote dreams of working with papooses seemed fearfully far away. Now Tokawaka reservation called me.

It was with quaking heart that I had started for the station. Since then everything had happened so quickly. A dizzy whirl of preparation; whizzing past miles and miles of open space; a long wait, half-cooked and smothery, alone on the sun-baked sidewalk outside the station in Saskatoon, Saskatchewan.

We whizzed westward, past miles of golden grain – life-giving food – waving in the wind and glistening in the sun. Then we chugged up rugged cliffs, where we watched a mountain goat balancing precariously on the rocks. Below, a moose grazed unconcernedly on the succulent grass. And, far below, at the bottom of the deep canyon was a roaring waterfall.

As I gazed on this changing panorama, I could picture the first North American Indians roaming through this beautiful country, free and independent. Something inside me clicked. I realised how these Indians must have felt – and still feel – confined on cramped reservations. After thousands of years of sole possession, they were relegated to being 'wards' of the government, regarded by many as second-class citizens. Seventy-four per cent of the Indians still live on reservations. Their lives are controlled by the government Department of Indian Affairs, who appoint local agents, hitherto always white men, to act as middle-men between the Government and each reservation. The policy of the Department is gradually to encourage the Indians to become self-supporting, leading eventually to complete integration with white society, but though they provide the Indians with the bare necessities of life with nursing, medical and schooling facilities, all too often little or nothing has been done to provide jobs for them, and with the decline of their traditional occupations of hunting and fishing, unemployment has risen until today it is a problem of the first magnitude.

From childhood, pictures and stories about papooses had fascinated me. Later I had read much about Indians getting a raw deal. I had heard the appeals of various church organizations for the great need of nursing services. But I was lethargic. The crisis came after I attended a public meeting, and heard the speaker talk about the unjust treatment of Indians by a negligent agent; about indifference, and of careless legislation. I itched to get first-hand knowledge, to learn whether or not eye-opener stories of startling incidents I had read in magazines and newspapers were really true.

Why did I, and other North Americans, consider ourselves superior to Indians who have played extremely important parts in opening the North American continent of today? Why, in a democratic country, should we have thousands of human beings, who live, laugh, and love as we do, yet do not have adult privileges in order to build better homes? Why did these first inhabitants of North America, men and women whose ancestors' dust mingled with the earth they loved in their own land, not have their freedom like I had? Why until recently were they an almost forgotten people within our borders?

I knew my conscience would never be satisfied until I could get first-hand experience. I realized that the change I was about to make would be a long jump from nursing in an organized hospital; from a good salary, to a mere pittance, and living among strangers who spoke another language. But after much soul-searching and prayer I was still willing to make the change.

In answer to my application, a month later I received a letter asking me to take charge of the health of Indians in this residential School on Tokawaka reservation.

I accepted.

I was brought back to reality as the captain shouted, 'All aboard'.

'Follow me,' muttered the steward.

We tagged behind him, staggered up the forty-five degree gangplank, swayed with unsteady legs along the deck, side-stepped boards, crates and drums, ducked down the stairway, and strode through a long passageway to cabins. Outside Number Four, the steward jangled his keys, stepped inside, plonked my grip on the floor, and exclaimed, 'Take your choice, upper or lower. You're first. Leaving shortly.'

I knew that coast water travel in small boats made it necessary to take everything into consideration. During a storm, port-holes of the upper can too generously spray the occupant with cold brine. Thankful to have first choice, I chose the lower. No other passenger came to occupy the upper, and I faced each morning dry and unscathed. Strange to say, 'leaving shortly,' actually meant shortly. The S.S. *Norah* swung from the deck, backed slowly out of the harbour, cleared the pier, and started her trip *en route* to Port Alice, passing Tokawaka, our destination, about half-way up the Pacific Coast.

Tarred rope, rattling chains, huge boxes, drums of gasoline, and fish cases scuttled about until bronzed sailors roped each article securely. The deck confusion gradually became less chaotic. We were off to our new adventure with Indians and the papooses. I watched Victoria fade slowly into a black spot. How much more would I know about Indians by this time the following year?

John Bell, eager to air his knowledge, interrupted my meditations. He told us that the *Norah* built in Scotland, was an extremely well-made boat, and left Victoria for Port Alice fortnightly, loaded with supplies and passengers calling at all the fishing ports *en route*.

'Most of the officers have names beginning with Mac, and they speak with a Scottish brogue. Here comes Captain Mac.'

Captain MacDonald, commonly called Captain Mac, gim-

13

leted us with narrowing eyes, as he exclaimed, 'Another nurse and school teachers! They do change often, and what a variety of characters we have toted to and from Tokawaka! Good trade for us, bad for the Indians! Hope you will like it. Beautiful scenery ahead; better stay on deck. Good sailors, eh? Fish up here are always hungry and optimistic – like the Indians.'

A twinkle in his sea-blue eyes, he chuckled to himself as he ducked down the ladder.

On the last day on board, the hoarse moaning of the foghorn echoed eerily across the water. Breaking waves swished and slapped the reefs. Huge combers lashed the sides of the steamer. Icy spray oozed through the ventilator. Rain pelted the deck in torrents. The salt air penetrated the marrow of our bones, and fog enveloped everything.

The briny odour played havoc with the chemical composition of my gastric juices. I huddled in a deck chair, wrapped in my heavy goat-skin coat. I had reached the limit of endurance when a sudden sideways roll followed a quick lurch forward. I gulped, swayed on unsteady legs, and heaved my preciously-hoarded supper to Captain Mac's optimistic fish. During the period of the ship's adjustment, my stomach seemed always to be coming up and flopping down. My rubbery legs wobbled as though on roller skates. By awful exertion, I managed to make the stairs, flopped on to my berth, grabbed my seasick cup, and crawled between the woollen blankets, fully clothed.

I could sympathize with Ellen, moaning and retching in the next cabin. Her plaintive voice wailed, 'History says that Indians in dugouts and canoes were good sailors, and that they could ride the waters unscathed and not be seasick. Why in a fairly comfortable boat do we have to endure this misery? Do you suppose it is the chiefs' spirits getting their revenge for whites taking their lands?'

The *Norah* chugged around a rugged cliff. Grey-winged sea gulls wheeling and winnowing about the deck like constant couriers screamed and mewed. Several porpoises zwanged up from the dark surface, curved above the waves for a few seconds, inhaled the necessary breath in perfect timing, and zipped beneath the surface.

The chief steward, Andy MacLean, strolled along and

pointed to a large, white building, high up on the cliff – like a sore thumb. He chuckled to himself, as he remarked, 'Aye, and that be your School. Rough seas and shallow water be a-making it impossible to land freight at Tokawaka. Three blasts notify your principal, Mr King' (under his breath, 'some man'), 'that we are steaming into John's Creek, three miles away, where he will meet you with the School boat, *Daybreak*.'

'So that's where we're going. Some smell, eh?' said John.

'You'll smell like that in a few weeks,' remarked Andy.

Ellen, accustomed to the smell of salt water, replied, 'Just Pacific brine.'

'Indians,' insisted Andy.

I recalled indescribable, unforgettable odours encountered on slimy, fishing stages at Rock End in the remote Magdalen Islands where I had once been posted.'* Somehow this pungent odour was vastly different. I recalled having heard that you could smell an Indian reservation long before you reached it.

The Indians I saw moving silently about the wharf intrigued me. The deck activities also fascinated us. Three hoarse blasts echoed across the salt water. The *Norah* smacked the pier. Sailors dashed here and there. One threw a lariat, straight as an arrow. An agile Indian on the wharf caught it deftly, ran and threw it over the bollard. The motor died. The boat quivered from stem to stern, settled quietly into the water, and I felt the engine vibrations quivering through my feet. Small boats, coming as if by magic from nowhere, chugged and putted across the water. They bumped the car-tyre shock-absorbers, making little dull thuds. Gulls, flapping their wings, uttering hoarse cries of derision, screamed hungrily as they swirled and looped above and around the *Norah*.

The loaded crane creaked slowly up from the mammoth hold, swung clear of the deck, an Indian unhooked the hasp, and beehive activity commenced. Indians, like bees buzzing about a honey pot, watched their precious food being unloaded, then gathered silently about their little heap of goods on the weather-worn boards. Dozens of small boats collected about

*See *Nurse of the Islands* (William Kimber.)

15

the sides of the steamer, adhering like barnacles. Men and boys swarmed the deck.

Women, with papooses spread-eagled on their backs, squatted on the rough, loose board wharf, guarding rows of extensively woven, coloured reed baskets and braided cedar mats. Older, half-naked button-eyed youngsters stood silently beside their mothers, oblivious to all self-consciousness.

Scratching, mangy dogs, beset with fleas, so thin they had to stand twice in the same place to see their shadows, tore at their bodies. Their paws kept up a continuous tattoo on the loose boards, adding to the excitement. I recalled someone saying, 'The good Lord gave dogs fleas to prevent them from having nervous breakdowns. They scratch off their surplus energy.'

'Any freight for Topsail, Big John?'

'Nope, not this trip.'

'Me, no money today, credit good, take it out of my next fish catch.'

'I can't. Bring fish, and I will give you credit.'

'That's all for the reservation. School boat next. Make way for the *Daybreak.*'

A short man with snapping, black eyes, twisted moustache, and coal-black hair, stepped up, and said, 'I presume you are all for the School. I am Mr King, the principal. Follow me.'

We tagged meekly behind him as he backed down the ladder into a small boat with a cabin, anchored to the *Norah,* with *Daybreak* painted in black letters on its white side.

'What about our baggage?' enquired John.

'Have to pull alongside the hatch for our freight,' replied Mr King.

'Isn't this Tokawaka?' asked Ellen.

Mr King raised his eyebrows, and replied, 'Whites live here. We live on the other side of the reservation.' Our first lesson.

I thought, 'Do we count as whites or Indians?' Nevertheless, I swung myself downward, with fearful misgivings, but I landed in the centre of the boat. Ellen jumped down beside me.

We began to realize that we knew little about Indians. Although curious I was reluctant to ask questions, and was glad when John asked, 'Do we live on the reservation?'

16

'We are whites. We live at the end of the boardwalk,' replied Mr King. The tone of his voice indicated, 'How stupid some intelligent people are.' And that was supposed to explain everything.

Mr King's five year old son, Tommy, told us. 'Indians cannot live with whites 'cause they are wards of the government.'

It was evident that one did not ask questions of this tight-lipped principal. One was expected to be dumb; knowledge would be imparted, learned by reading, or by hard experience. Mr King had lived so long among Indians, he had acquired their characteristic silence.

'That's all for the School,' announced the purser.

The *Norah's* propeller churned the water.

Mr King shouted to another son, 'Bill, start the engine.'

The *Daybreak* swung away from the wharf. We did not dare ask what water we were crossing, but eventually Mr King announced, 'John's Creek.'

Of course. Andy had mentioned that we would have to cross this creek. Was it the name of a village, or was the water named after some prominent man? Much later, we learned that it was just a name for the water that separated the white man's pier from the Indian reservation wharf, up which we had to climb to pass through their village, *en route* to the School. No one could recall any person named John sufficiently prominent to have a creek named after him.

The moment the *Daybreak* bumped a wobbly, slimy fishing stage, Mr King blew a shrill blast on his whistle. Ten mahogany-coloured broad-shouldered Indian boys popped out of shacks on the nearby reservation, ran nimbly along the rickety, board sidewalk, and shinned down the ladder into our boat.

'Tide's low, you will have to hike the rest of the way through the village and over the boardwalk,' remarked Mr King.

'Boardwalk! Like New York! Better than I anticipated! Tokawaka City here we come,' whispered John.

Each boy shouldered a piece of freight and scrambled up the stage ladder. Without asking more foolish questions, we clambered up the ladder rungs. As I sniffed the foul-smelling air, John said, 'Sure, it's Indians.'

I recalled my hostile reception when I returned home from

B   17

working on fishing boats on the Atlantic Coast. Relatives sniffed around me, insisting that I smelled too fishy. They made me hang my clothes outside before they would accept me. Thus, I had a premonition that my clothing would be burned this time before they would accept me into their houses. Never having visited an Indian reservation, they would never appreciate the pleasant odour any more than a farmer accepts and appreciates a skunk's hospitable fragrance.

We threaded our way behind Mr King through the village, along the hard-beaten path, interspersed with oozy cow pats. At the opposite edge of the village, he stopped, and said, 'Watch your step. The boardwalk is mighty slippery at this time of the year.'

Two ten-inch planks, nailed side by side, were strung on posts six feet above swampy ground.

'Boardwalk,' exclaimed Ellen. 'I was expecting something like New York's Boardwalk.'

'Here's for the straight and narrow path,' said John, and strode ahead. Ellen gathered her skirts about her, and put one foot gingerly on the centre of the plank. With trepidation in my heart, I slid my feet cautiously along the green moss, which oozed over the edges of the planks; all the time wondering if my old rubbers would protect me.

Half-way along, without taking his eyes from his feet, John said, 'We'll be mountain goats or tight-rope walkers before we know it!'

After skidding over this moss-grown boardwalk for a quarter of a mile, we came out of the woods close to the School, which loomed large at the end of the walk.

'There she is!' exclaimed John. 'Take a good look! That School may be the turning point of our lives!'

'Or the end,' added Ellen.

There seemed to be hundreds of beady, black eyes peering at us from the School windows and around corners. Actually, only sixty-odd pairs of curious eyes in children's faces, gazing at us. Eyes of children with affection-starved hearts, trying to get a glimpse of their supplementary mothers – new teachers and nurse.

Every detail of those first moments on the boardwalk, at the threshold of the School, where we were about to enter our new adventure with Indians, became deeply imprinted on my mind. Those brown-skinned, almond-shaped eyed girls and boys, wards of the government, children of North American pioneers, spent the formative years of their lives in the School segregated a quarter of a mile from parents and relatives. They were always under the supervision and at the mercy of one or more white staff members.

There was no turning back. The next moment I would plunge into the starting point of a long visualized dream. Life might never be the same. Now that the actual moment to open the door had come, trepidation made me doubt the wisdom of my decision. My legs felt like jelly-fish; butterflies no longer fluttered about my stomach, they were on the wing.

Although eager to start working with these papooses, I dreaded to leave the boardwalk and open that door.

CHAPTER 2

I MEET THE PAPOOSES

Mr King had stalked ahead muttering, 'Must tend to my stack of mail. Go in.' He had continued on to the principal's residence, leaving us like lone orphans, wondering what was expected from us.

'What a welcome!' exclaimed John.

Ellen, craning her neck to see through a crack in the curtain, asked, 'What do you suppose is waiting inside?'

John threw back his head, puffed out his chest, and said, 'Who's afraid of the Big, Bad Wolf. No one is going to eat us.' He took the plunge, turned the knob, stepped inside, and we trailed behind him.

A bleary-eyed woman, with straggly hair, and down-at-the-heel slippers, shuffled along the hall. She extended a limp hand, and in a lifeless voice, said, 'Glad to know you. I am Bridget Blakely, the kitchen matron.'

Although her voice lacked enthusiasm, this was our first real welcome. Considering her ordeal ended, she said to a teenage Indian girl, 'Bertha, don't stand gawking. Show these workers to their rooms, and mind you come right back and tend to your chores.'

We followed Bertha, like three blind mice, up rickety stairs. She paused at the first landing and announced, 'Mr Bell, you sleep here. Miss Banfill, you sleep there. Miss Morris, you sleep higher up.'

John whispered, 'They even know our names. I bet they know all about us; have discussed what we will be like, where we come from, why we are here, and I expect they even know our ages.'

'Bertha, come down this minute,' shouted Mrs Blakely.

'Maybe she's afraid of what Bertha's telling us,' said John.

20

Ellen came down, glanced about, and remarked, 'Our rooms seem to have gone to seed, like the rest of the building, and Mrs Blakely, if she is an example of the staff.'

The acrid odour of unwashed bodies and the smell of un-ventilated, old buildings, mingled with cooking odours, wafted up the open stairway. A wet mop had been swashed about the centre of the floors, missing by accident or design damp, matted dirt wads, which formed wedges in corners where the boards met. My bedroom was sandwiched between two hall dormitories. The back door opened into an entry-way, which led to the girls' hospital room on one side and the boys' on the other, with a peep hole in each door. Another door in my bedroom opened into the hall at the top of the stairway opposite John's bedroom.

The loud clanging of a bell echoed through the building, and Mrs Blakely shouted upstairs, 'That means dinner, and Mr King, he be mighty particular about "punctility".'

I think we all felt nervous at what we had taken on, though had we suspected half of the complexities ahead of us, we would have been bushed before we started!

The senior boys and girls, brought back from summer vacation at the canneries, had scrubbed the school and cooked the children's first meal. But this was the term's official opening day. Before midday the smaller children had to be at the School. Matrons and older girls had spent hours scrubbing the youngsters, fine-combing their hair, issuing new clothing, and destroying old clothing, which had been worn at home or in the canneries.

Mr King, ramrod straight, motioned for us to take our places on his left. Pointing to a woman on his right, he said, 'My wife, the matron; Mrs Blakely, the kitchen matron, and Mrs Grimsby, our sewing matron.'

We stood waiting, rather like prize animals at a country fair, waiting to be judged.

'All right, Stella,' snapped Mr King.

A fifteen year old girl sauntered over, unhooked the door on the boys' side of the room. An endless stream of copper-skinned boys, with soap-glistening faces and wet-plastered hair, fell through the door. They scooted to their familiar stalls at the

21

tables, and stood behind long, wooden benches, waiting for a signal from Mr King.

Stella unlocked a door on the opposite side of the room, and girls, in checked, blue-and-white gingham aprons and light tan running shoes, scuffed along and took their places behind the benches. I learned in time that Indian girls and women scuff or shuffle along. Boys and men, accustomed to walking on long trails, walk more gracefully.

The children, wearing their best behaviour manners, concentrated their attention on Mr King and the new staff members. (Later, we learned they had been bribed by a nickel apiece for the occasion.)

Mr King had barely pronounced the Amen in Grace, when, as though timed, each child raised a leg and started to swing it over the bench. One scathing glance from Mr King changed their minds. Legs were quickly and quietly drawn back, reminding me of cringing puppies. Mr King waited. Shoulders straightened, like those of soldiers facing inspection. When one could hear a pin drop, he announced, 'Boys and girls, this is Miss Morris, Mr Bell, and Miss Banfill.'

The moment the slowest child had settled himself on his bench, Mr King announced, 'You may eat.'

Their ordeal ended, sixty-four bodies had followed those legs over the benches and squeezed into allotted places along the long benches. Tongues ceased to lick lips. Every child waded into generous servings of boiled potatoes, raw carrots, and boiled cod fish. Knives and forks clicked against plates. Mrs Grimsby paced back and forth behind the long rows of children, her eagle eye making certain that each child got an equal share of the food – like a farmer watching pigs' troughs to make certain that runts get their fair share. Later, I learned that scraps could be tucked under the table, or they could be thrown across the room, in the flick of an eyelid.

We went through the kitchen to the staff dining-room. Our first, by far not the last, association with those body-food-odour-flea-infested dining-rooms.

Twice a day, during the following months, I walked along behind the long rows of papooses. When the slowest eating child swallowed his last mouthful of food, each child tipped back his head and opened his mouth. As I dropped the allotted, compulsory dose of cod-liver oil into those gaping mouths, I felt like a mother robin. I could never figure how long it actually took that awful stuff to trickle down the long red tube to the already stuffed stomachs.

Officials of the Department of Indian Affairs had given in-structions that each child must be given this oil, from November to April or longer, according to weather and the health of the children. By spring, the children and I smelled like a cod-liver oil rendering plant. Most of the children accepted this oil as part of their education and daily routine. However, fifteen year old Lena, obese and intelligent, having read in a magazine that girls should have slender waists (unusual with many Indian women), rebelled. Eventually, she decided that cod-liver oil was preferable to punishment for disobedience – the lesser of two evils. She would shut her eyes and swallow the stuff.

The first day, four year old Freddie clenched his teeth and refused to open his lips. I heard Paul whisper, 'You'll catch it!' He was such a baby, I did not have the heart to hold him, force it down, or to report to Mr King, who no doubt would have strapped him. In less than a week, he tipped back his head, opened his mouth, and said, 'Me's ready, my's candy.'

Later we followed Mr King into the sitting-room, and he said, 'Sit.' He stood, twiddling his moustache, gimleted his gaze on John's face, and continued, 'For your edification, you have to understand our routine. The officials of the Department of Indian Affairs require every Indian child, six years old and over, able to pass a medical examination, to be taken from his or her home environment, and admitted into my School, or to the Roman Catholic School. Should a father or mother like me, I do not adhere strictly to government regulations. I have accepted Freddie, four, and Jeannie, five years old, for this term. Their parents thought that I could teach them better than they could teach them at home.'

Much later we learned that Freddie's mother was expecting a baby. Her husband was away fishing. Along with two younger children, she could not control him, and so they decided to send him to the School. Jeannie's parents, recent graduates of

23

the School, loved their children. However, they thought that she could be taught more niceties of life in the School, which would be beneficial to her in later life, than they could give or teach her at home.

Mr King continued, 'You can see, I give the children good food and provide them with the necessities of life until they are sixteen years old. Nurse, under me, you must keep the children healthy.'

He drew his short stature to full height, and continued, 'Miss Morris, under me, you are responsible for the education of the senior grades, and Mr Bell, the juniors. I am too busy today to explain your other obligations to me, and to the School.'

He threw back his shoulders, puffed up like an adder, and said, 'You understand that I am the principal.' We understood.

Ellen rose calmly to the occasion, and said, 'We certainly appreciate your thoughtfulness, and will do anything we can to help your children.'

The moment he left us, John slumped into his chair, and exclaimed, 'We're in for it!'

We just sat, staring at each other. Everything was so different to the glowing reports, which we had read in church papers. Eventually Ellen came to, and remarked, 'Now, I know why Captain Mac had the quizzical look in his eyes, when he said, "They do change often".'

A damper checked our enthusiasm for helping papooses, and we slunk upstairs. We flopped on to John's bed, humble and fearful. Yesterday strangers, today sympathy for Indians and a craving for fellowship drew us together in a common bond.

Ellen echoed my thoughts, when she said, 'I am going to need help to stand by my moral convictions, let's stick together.'

I replied, 'I can put up with a lot but I intend to live my Christianity not just teach it.'

Mr King had informed me that I must examine every child before he or she entered the class room. So I enquired into details and discovered that at the opening of each term every child had to be examined. When the children returned from vacations, such examinations were absolutely essential. It was evident that previous examinations had been of a brief nature.

Each newly admitted child had to have a thorough examination; later be taken across the channel for a medical examination.

Mrs Grimsby and the older girls had unmercifully scrubbed bodies and searched heads for hopping-crawlers. It was my duty to check for infections, impetigo, venereal sores, colds, or coughs, which the children might have contracted. I also had to watch for signs of tuberculosis, venereal, and other infectious symptoms, which might cause an epidemic.

When the children had finished their dishes and other chores, I went to the dispensary. They were lined up like soup-kitchen customers. The older children were not frightened, having gone through this process yearly. But they were eager to size up the new nurse, and to test or confuse her with their real or imaginary sores. The newcomers hung back, not from fear of the nurse, because they had seen nurses about the village. Their eyes were wide with wonder. In one hour, while daubing iodine on real or fanciful cuts, covering running sores with ointment, etc., I learned more about papooses than I had during my entire life time.

Snapping-eyed Jeannie began to whimper, hung back, and clung to her sister, Sheila. She shoved her through the door, admonishing. 'Go in. She's not going to hurt you.' Although Jeannie did not understand much English, or know what to expect, she had learned that she must do what the other children did. She came into the dispensary, opened wide her mouth, stuck out her tongue, shoved up her sleeve, and let me examine her. All the time, her eyes were darting about watching my every movement. The moment she saw the thermometer she closed her lips as tightly as a vice, and refused to open them.

Sheila came to my help, and said, 'If I could explain, in Indian, what you want to do, she will let you put the thermometer into her mouth. But we are punished if we speak Indian in the School or on the campus.'

I looked at that tiny, frightened papoose, with fast-beating heart and tight lips, thought of Mr King's warning, 'I make all the rules.' Then I recalled my first day at school, and said, 'Tell her in Indian what I want her to do.'

Sheila spoke a few words, and Jeannie's bright eyes twinkled.

25

She looked up at me and said, 'I 'member, Nurse Berry, did it when I little,' she flashed me one of her quick sweet smiles which we soon learned to expect when she was pleased with anything, which was most of the time. Her smiles won the hearts of all the staff members, and she could easily have been spoiled, but it was not fair to show favouritism.

Freddie hung back until Jimmy, his older brother, picked him up and carried him, like a seal, screaming at the top of his voice, into the dispensary. Jimmy explained, 'He is not afraid of you. He is afraid you are going to put him into the bath tub again. Martha said that it took three of them to hold him in the tub this afternoon.'

Freddie must have had a frightful experience with a tub, no doubt in babyhood. Out in the salt water he was like a young seal, not frightened of anything. There was nothing seriously wrong with most of the children. But it did not require a professional eye to detect Freddie's running nose and other abnormal outward symptoms, indicative of venereal disease. Any lay person could see that ten year old Nixon had some chronic disease and should have a thorough medical examination and extra attention. School routine required me to take the newly admitted children across the channel for a doctor's examination. So I decided to add Nixon's name to the list and let the doctor decide the diagnosis for both children.

A bell clanged through the School. John, trying without much success to concentrate on preparing lessons for the first day of teaching, stuck his head out of the door, and enquired, 'Suppose we eat again? I am starving.' Licking our lips in anticipation, we went downstairs. Mr and Mrs King, Mrs Blakely, and Mrs Grimsby were lined up against the wall, and the children were wiggling into their stalls.

Mr King announced, 'Prayers.'

Every head bowed instantly, and over sixty voices rattled through The Lord's Prayer. Curiosity predominated in my mind. I played truant and looked straight into Freddie's wondering eyes. He wrinkled his nose, peered at me, and his funny, old-man face took on one of his face-covering grins, which we learned to expect any moment. He seemed to be asking, 'What's it all about?'

26

Prayers ended. A moment of silence. The children's eyes sought Mr King's face expectantly. He gave them his regular fifteen minute nightly oration on obedience to the staff, good manners to everyone at all times, the necessity of duties well done, and loyalty to him. Then, he allotted them their routine morning duties, turned to the staff, and announced, 'Mrs Grimsby, you will have charge of the girls tonight. Mr Bell, you will take charge of the boys and see that they are all in bed and lights out at nine o'clock.'

I heard John mutter, 'So soon! What do you suppose I have to do? Kiss them all good night?'

Although this was his first teaching position, he rose to the situation, and said, 'Come boys,' and led the way out of the room. The girls followed Mrs Grimsby out the other door. At nine-thirty, John came upstairs, flopped on to his bed, and exclaimed, 'That's over! Am I well initiated! The boys did not let me down. They told me what I had to do.'

Before the children quietened down in the older girls' dormitory, I heard Martha whisper, 'Freddie, blow your nose and stop sniffling.'

John told us that when he had them all safely tucked into cots, Sammy had whispered, 'Were we good enough to get the nickel Mr King promised each of us if we would act our best tonight?'

Such a whirl of new experiences. It was impossible to digest all that had happened. Everything was so different to what we had expected. The thought of braving the village on the morrow and trying to find my way alone among people in their different homes, where most of the women would not be able to understand me, almost floored me.

John yawned and said, 'I have had my quota for one day! I am dead tired! Puppets we are, so let's away to bed. The strings may be pulled too early tomorrow.'

CHAPTER 3

GETTING TO KNOW YOU

They were indeed. Too soon, a clanging bell wakened me. Hubbub below, scurrying feet in the next room, and Martha's, 'Freddie, blow your nose,' enlightened me. I snapped awake. This was my new adventure.

It was the duty of older children to make certain that each child got out of his bed, rolled his bedclothes back to air, scrubbed his face and cleaned his teeth, before the breakfast bell rang. A lull in the noise was followed by, 'Freddie, get out of those pyjamas immediately, and I mean hurry.'

'What?' lisped Freddie.

'Pyjamas! Those things!' explained Martha.

Having slept nude or in his day clothes, pyjamas were the same as pants to Freddie. Although he could not understand much English, by the tone of Martha's voice, he knew that she meant hurry.

'Getting,' he lisped.

In a sterner voice, Martha said, 'Freddie, the bell will ring shortly, and you will not get anything to eat. Come here at once and let me see if you have washed your face.'

Routine face washing was a new experience for him. But, with a young robin stomach, he knew what the word eating meant.

'Coming,' he lisped, and scooted to the bathroom for inspection.

Sheila was trying to initiate Jeannie into School routine; jabbering in English and Indian. 'Wash tomorrow. Don't need now!' replied Jeannie.

The clatter of granite dishes and silverware in the kitchen and dining-room, beneath my room, indicated that the girls, whom Mr King had allotted for breakfast duty, were doing their duties with a vengeance – setting, or throwing, dishes and silverware

28

about the children's tables. In the basement, garbage tins banged noisily. Ashes were being shaken down with unnecessary vigour. Older boys were making certain that they would not miss their breakfast.

In an amazingly quick time, all the children were lined up outside the two dining-room doors.

The older children had learned from experience that a missed breakfast was a reality. During the first weeks, Freddie heard, 'Blow your nose,' so much that whenever he met one of the staff, he would grin from ear to ear, and lisp, 'Did blow.' This was one of his first English sentences.

The previous evening, Sheila had informed me that 'Nurses always have dispensary hours right after breakfast and right after supper.' Morning prayers ended. I went to the dispensary, where I was kept busy daubing iodine or ointment on real or imaginary sores and cuts until the two class room bells called all the children, with the exception of Freddie, to classes or to work outside. The class rooms, with new teachers, gave promise of more excitement than cuts.

With the exit of over sixty children, a strange hush settled about the huge building. I started to pack my village nursing bag, with many misgivings. The door opened suddenly, and Mr King stalked in, like a chief surgeon entering an operating-room. He muttered, 'Good morning,' peered into my bag, and said, 'I always check all my staff's work and the medicine for difficult cases.'

I thought he was joking, so I asked, 'Have you a licence to handle drugs?'

He threw back his head, his cheeks twitched, his eyes snapped, he put his hands in his pockets, and strutted about the office. 'I am the principal here. The Indians do what I say and take what I order.'

A quirk in my make-up rebelled. What had I let myself in for? Take orders from a lay person, yet be held responsible for the proper use of drugs and treatment of Indians.

He continued, 'Naturally, as I am responsible for the health of all Indians here, I want to know what any nurse prescribes.'

I had been engaged to take charge of the health of these Indians and had hoped for co-operation and help from the principal and matron. It was evident that I would have to take a definite stand or be a door-mat. Although my throat muscles tightened, I managed to keep my voice sufficiently level to reply, 'Although you may be the principal, I am responsible for the drugs and the nursing. I realize that you have had much more experience with Indians than I have had and I will be grateful to you for advice regarding any problems which are new to me. Here is my letter of appointment, it definitely states that I am to have charge of their health.'

Luckily I had brought my appointment letter into the dispensary. I read to him, 'The nurse shall be responsible for the health of the children in the School, Indians on the reservation, and shall have charge of the dispensary.'

'I am the only one with any authority here,' he shouted, went out, banged the door so hard the whole building shook.

As I listened to his heels working off some of his anger, my knees went limp. Winged butterflies whirred in my stomach. Some of the glow of my early dreams vanished. I prayed for strength to face the problems ahead.

I was brought back to reality by a faint tapping on the dispensary door, like a bird pecking on a limb. I opened the door. Freddie stood outside looking more forlorn than I felt. He reminded me of a little pebble on a vast beach, a pathetic mite, too small to go into the class-room, not wanted at home or in the sewing-room with Mrs Grimsby and the older girls. Considered a nuisance by the older boys outside, and put out of the kitchen, he did not know what to do. Then he must have remembered the touch of affection received the previous evening, and found his way to the dispensary to help the nurse.

He lisped, 'Freddie help, blow nose.'

I pointed to my bag, and said, 'Village.'

He grinned from ear to ear, and said, 'Go.'

'No, Freddie, not this time.'

A dejected look passed over his little old-man face and I wanted to cry.

He smiled and lisped, 'Freddie, go village, blow nose heaps.'

My heart ached for this mere baby in his loneliness. I longed to sit down, take him on my knee and cuddle him, but I was already late starting for the village. What could I do with

30

him? Then I had an idea. I took his hand and we found a large
bottle with a small neck, spoon, and a tin cup. I led him to a
sandy spot, pointed to the sand and the bottle, showed him how
to fill it, and said, 'Freddie fill. Nurse go village. Freddie fill
high. Nurse come back.' He watched every movement closely.
Satisfied that he was helping, he grinned, and continued to
scoop up the sand. This would keep him busy until recess, when
he could play with the other children. I slipped away to the
village with a lighter heart.

It was a lovely September morning. Birds cheeped overhead.
A short distance from the boardwalk, gentle waves lapped the
beach. I walked through the woods, trying to picture what it
would be like in the Indians' homes.

A soothing wind, stirring through the furze, calmed my
troubled mind. As I drew near the reservation, my steps grew
shorter and my pace slower. One look at the wooden shacks at
the end of the boardwalk made me pause, and pray for strength
to know what to say, and what to do.

Lena Paul, a School graduate, answered my first knock with
'Come in.' I entered and said, 'Good morning.'

Lena replied, 'Hallo.'

My tongue remained glued to the roof of my mouth. Lena
did not ask me to sit or appear to want to talk.

'Are you all well?' I asked.

She replied, 'I am alone. Both of my children are in your
School, and George is out fishing.'

I seemed to detect resentment in her voice. Was it because
her children had been taken from her, or was it because I was
inspecting her home? I asked, 'Who lives next door?'

'Skookum Annie. Go around to the back,' she replied. Skookum was the prefix meaning old, I learned.

I knocked. There was no answer. After the third knock I
heard a sort of guttural grunt, which I took to be a friendly
welcome. 'Good morning,' I said.

An old woman, with leather-like face, squatting in the centre
of what appeared to have been an old smoke house, gazed
steadily at me through half-closed eyes, but did not speak.

'Are you well?' brought no answer.

'Do you live alone?' Still no response.

31

The constant stare was creepy. As I went out of the door, I sensed eyes boring through my back, and heard her muttering unintelligible words in Indian, presumably 'Goodbye' or 'Good riddance.'

I was given a warm reception at the next home. Gladys, a recent graduate, opened the door with a cheery, 'Good morning, Nurse, glad to see you. How are Charlie and Janet at the School?' She did not wait for a reply, but continued, 'This is four year old Dixon, and Peter, two. Will you sit? I saw you coming from Skookum Annie's home. She is blind and does not speak or understand English.'

So that explained the silence and boring eyes.

I walked on and on through the barren, almost ghostlike village. An old crippled Indian grunted a greeting. An English-speaking young woman chatted. A pre-school child stood and stared. I reached the last home, mentally and physically exhausted. I drew a deep sigh of relief at being back on the boardwalk, with time to ponder my strange morning experiences. It seemed so senseless, with no one sick, for a nurse to trudge about to every home each morning. My ignorance of Indians and their customs prevented me from realizing why it was necessary for a nurse to visit each home daily.

Freddie, sitting on the dispensary doorsteps, grinning from ear to ear, greeted me like a long, lost sister. He held up a full bottle of sand, and lisped, 'Freddie fill.'

I had not the heart to say, 'Blow your nose.'

During lunch, Mr King asked, 'Have many Indians returned from fishing?' So that was the reason for the ghostlike village.

During the week I continued my education, for I learned why this visiting was so important. Many aches, pains, infected eyes, and injured fingers, which might have been neglected, were discovered in the early stage, preventing much sickness. Still later, to my sorrow, I learned another important reason for my daily visiting.

One morning, after I had tramped through this empty village every day for three weeks, Gladys said, 'Tomorrow, most of our people will return from the canneries and from fishing. The other nurses visited this end of the village first one morning, starting at different homes each morning. You know we have to keep our houses clean for daily inspection, and you have to report any signs of whisky or drunkenness on the reservation.'

No one had been kind enough to enlighten me, or even drop a hint, that I had this extra responsibility. I wondered if I was supposed to be a policeman as well as a nurse, and why I had not been informed about this unpleasant task.

The next morning, I set out with my bag, hoping to find some real nursing. My heart was happy and I was eager to meet the Indians. The reservation was no longer a ghost town. Men, women, old, and young, little children, dogs, fleas and flies swarmed everywhere. Men were squatting in little groups on the stages, all talking at once in Indian. Women with babies in arms and youngsters spread-eagled on backs, had congregated in homes. Children crawled about among feather ticks, chamber pots, frying pans, dried clams, smoked fish, dirty clothes, and rubber boots. Everything had been dumped on the floors, just as they had brought them from their boats. I found that time, in the sense of measuring its duration by clocks and days of the week, meant nothing to them. Now was the time to talk over what had happened at the various fishing grounds and canneries; get news from relatives, loaf, and smoke. Time would stand still. A big feast would be held. Then they would have most of the winter to sort through their personal belongings.

A copper-faced Indian, with a long scar running diagonally across one cheek, met me, and announced, 'I am Chief Kenderson. How are my boys Charles and Wilbur? They are all I have. Their mother died when Wilbur was four years old. Take good care of them.'

I had never encountered such a jumble of names, and soon gave up trying to list all the children under their parents' names. Skookum Job, Thomas Charlie, Charlie Frank, Skookum Peters, Frank Peters, Charlie David, David Charlie, and Paul August all looked alike. Still later I learned that many Indians discarded their first names. Others retained them, added a name or two or changed their first names to suit the occasion. A father might have a vivid dream about a beaver or seal and give his newborn son one of these names. Many of the boys, old enough to be classed as young men, were called after some deed which their fathers thought outstanding in the community – Bold, Brave, Hero, or Daring. As though this was not sufficiently confusing, many had taken their parents' surnames. Most of them had also adopted a white man's name, and dropped the surname, or tacked it on, and used it when emergency arose. I had many bewildering weeks before I learned the reasons for such a mix-up situation.

Visiting on the reservation, I would say, 'Good morning, Charlie Frank.'

Without a smile, the man would reply, 'I am Frank Charlie.'

The next time, sure of myself, I greeted a man with, 'Good day, George Thomas.'

He replied, 'I am Foster Thomas.'

It was not all my stupidity, because practically all the Indians had two different Indian and two white names. I had to learn the hard way. Eventually the jig-saw began to take on new meaning, and become less senseless, though more complex. I never did get all their names tagged to the right persons, but I soon identified faces.

These Indians, having worked hard all summer, needed a rest and relaxation. They returned from fishing or working in the canneries with a small amount of money or credit at their disposal. The Department of Indian Affairs and the Church bore the expense of nursing and medical care, and the upkeep and clothing for the children over six years of age; they provided the old people with ration slips, blankets and boards for funeral boxes. So Indians did not have to exert themselves to meet any of these expenses. This environment naturally enough did not have the best influence on their morales. These once self-supporting Indians, with so much time on their hands, developed a kind of native sluggishness, not really laziness. It was paradise for a white bootlegger who hung about the coast. He anchored just outside the shoreling limits, and after dark tempted the Indians who were looking for some means of enjoyment and relaxation.

It took some time for me to differentiate between a sniff of frowsy Indian odour and fermented home brew. It did not take long to learn which Indians resented being supervised by a young, white nurse, and which ones welcomed my inspections

34

and suggestions. Some women had a habit of tucking things out of sight when they saw me approaching.

And how could I lay a charge against George Thomas only to have him plead, 'Not guilty, I am John Thomas?'

I returned to the School each day wiser, bewildered and exhausted, and discussed the situation with the teachers who were having similar name-trouble with their pupils.

I began to wonder how long I would last. What would be my fate?

The day came when I had to make a list of the new children to take across to Dr Provost, appointed by the Department of Indian Affairs. He reserved one afternoon a month to examine six School children. Positive that ten year old Nixon had sugar diabetes, I added his name to my list. When Mr King checked the list, he exclaimed, 'There are six newcomers and Nixon is not a newly admitted child. Take his name off the list. There is nothing wrong with him but stupidity and laziness. He is an orphan, spoiled by his grandparents.'

I was determined to stand my ground, and replied, 'I have reason to believe that Nixon has a chronic disease that should have immediate treatment. Let us check his last medical report on your files.'

'No need to do that. My predecessor said that he had whipped, starved, threatened, and given him pills. He is just too lazy to get up at night. I have tried everything, but he still wets the bed. No use wasting the doctor's time and Mission money on him.'

'I am entitled to see his medical reports on your file. I would like to take them to the doctor.'

He stirred through an untidy mess of yellow papers, and brought out a file of medical reports and records. After much humming and hawing, he admitted that he could not find any medical report of Nixon ever having been examined. He muttered, 'Incomplete record. The last nurses must have been inefficient. Don't blame me.'

When he could not produce any record, I left Nixon's name on the list. The moment the doctor saw him, he roared, 'Why was this child not brought to me long ago?'

'Don't blame me,' I replied. 'He has been in the School four years, but there are no records of a previous examination. So I brought him across in order that you could check your records on him and give him another examination.'

He fumbled about among a stack of mussed papers, but was not able to produce any record of ever having examined him. 'Too late!' he exclaimed. 'Definitely a diabetic. An interesting case, because I have never seen an Indian with diabetes. I doubt if he will live to be twenty. Don't blame me. I did not know the child existed.'

'I am willing to give him insulin and special care,' I suggested.

'It would do more harm than good to start insulin. There is no one, during the summer, at the canneries, to give him hypodermics."

'Is there nothing that I can do to help him?'

'Absolutely nothing we can do. Nature may perform a cure, but I doubt it.'

At that time Indians could not be trusted with insulin, to give hypodermics regularly, and to watch for dangerous symptoms, which would require emergency treatment. It is said that syphilis was introduced to Indians by white people. It had been transmitted to Freddie and Jeannie, newly admitted children, little more than babies. The doctor examined them, and told me to bring them across for weekly treatment. Although these diseases could be arrested, it would effect their lives in many ways.

After discussing the School situation with the doctor, who also had his private practice, I left with a feeling of greater helplessness and frustration. He showed little interest in the improvement of the lot of the Indians, who were almost completely ignorant of the necessary, modern standards of hygienic health and prophylactic measures. Yet they were under his jurisdiction.

I was astonished at Mr King's reaction to Dr Provost's diagnosis of Nixon. Tears came into his eyes, and he said, 'Poor child! To think what he has gone through, and he could not help being a bed-wetter.' Then he added, 'Don't blame me. I am not responsible for the health of the children. Why did not the last three nurses or Dr Provost see that he was ill?' I thought, 'Passing the buck,' like soldiers in the army.

36

Mr Brant, the local agent, the only person able to act for these Indians, shrugged his shoulders, and replied, 'What's the use sending him away. He's only an Indian.'

Freddie and Jeannie would be treated. Nixon, doomed to an early death, would have to trust to Providence for relief. I was determined, over my dead body, that this much-abused child would not be punished any more for something over which he had no control. I would make certain that he would no longer have to sit with longing eyes and parched mouth watching the other children drink their bedtime cocoa.

Anyone who knows anything about diabetes, will realise what effect this had on his system and morale – and he did not have a father, mother, or social worker to see that he got justice.

CHAPTER 4

SUNDAY IN TOKAWAKA

On Sundays the rising bell rang one hour later than on week-days. On my first Sunday there, I shook myself awake for I was curious to participate in an Indian church service. While I was dressing, I heard loud sobbing, opened my door, and Jeannie, sitting on the lower stair with a woebegone expression on her face, was sobbing loudly. Large tears rolled from her usually sparkling eyes, as she sobbed, 'Lace, can't find.'

I produced a shoe lace and she rewarded me with one of her special smiles. Jeannie went to church. A loud howl from the dormitory, associated with Freddie, was followed by nose blowing. Martha was making certain that his nose would remain clean until they reached the church door, where she would repeat the nose wringing.

I went through to the dormitory where Stella and Martha, trying to get dressed, were overseeing the younger girls, who were scurrying in all directions, hunting for last minute pieces of Sunday clothing. I heard Stella exclaim, 'Beatrice, for goodness sake, can't you stand still? Hopping about like a rabbit, how do you expect me to button the back of your dress? The bell will ring any moment and you will be left behind.'

The bell rang, and Stella cried, 'Don't tell me that you have lost your church sweater again. How many times have I told you to hang it up in its proper place when you take it off? Hurry!'

Beatrice started to cry, but Jeannie put her arms around her shoulders, and said, 'Quick, hunt, most put here.' She lifted Beatrice's pillow and with shining eyes shouted, 'Here.'

'When you come home from church you hang that sweater in its proper place,' admonished Stella.

Beatrice had shown me the pretty, red sweater her mother had brought her for her birthday, and when I recalled my childhood I realised that the pillow, near her heart, was the logical place for her mother's present.

Mrs Grimsby shouted up, 'Everybody ready?' The girls went, helter-skelter, downstairs out to the walk, where John was waiting with the boys, lined up in single file.

'All your girls here, Miss Morris?'

'Martha, Stella, Lucy, Lena, Jeannie' on and on until each child had answered.

'Straighten up, Freddie. Pull in your chin, stick out your chest like a man. Ready, start.' John headed the boys' procession. Mrs Grimsby and the girls next, with Ellen as chaperone. The rest of the staff brought up the rear.

Right, left, right, left, the boardwalk vibrated like a bridge under a marching army. In order to prevent any child vanishing into his home, the children always marched double file through the village to the church at the far edge of the reservation. At the church door, Martha hauled Freddie aside and nearly twisted his nose off his face.

The boys glided silently, with sheep-like submission, down the aisle into front pews on the east side of the church. Grandfathers and fathers were sitting directly behind the boys, their corrugated, mask-like faces shining from much soap washing. The girls, with Freddie in tow, scuffed along to the front pews on the west side. Directly behind them, broad-beamed, well-cushioned mothers and grandmothers had waited an hour or two just to be near their children. These Indians, separated like sheep from goats, never enjoyed the satisfaction derived by a whole family sitting together in their own pews.

Above the sharp and acrid smell of children, I caught whiffs of that odour peculiar to Indians. I recalled a remark made by David Livingstone. He is reported to have said that when he first worked with Africans their keen sense of smell detected the white man's odours, which made them sick to their stomachs. Even though these white men bathed frequently and were themselves unconscious of any odour, I wondered if these Indians disliked odours exuding from our bodies.

These bright-eyed girls, alive with curiosity, watched every movement in front of them. The older Indians obviously derived much satisfaction and pleasure from the sonorous, droning words of Mr King. They sang or hummed the hymns with much gusto. Most of these Indians loved church services. Adults were interested, children docile. All nature seemed hushed and contented. Waves lapped the beach gently.

Mr King's voice ceased. My mind jerked back to reality and to the solemn-eyed children sitting so quietly in the stiff pews. The room was so still the fall of a pin would have startled a deaf person. He lifted the red christening bowl from the platform, and announced, 'We will baptize Mrs Tilliconce's baby.'

The children squirmed with excitement and anticipation. Beatrice nudged Jeannie. Sheila leaned over, scowled, shushed her, and whispered something to Martha. Ellen went back to the organ, which she had played during hymn singing. Mrs Tilliconce, bouncing her two months' old roly-poly, black-haired baby, got slowly to her feet. When she handed him to Mr King he was still jumping about like a monkey on a string. He dipped his fingers in the red bowl, let them drip over the baby's long, straight hair, and chanted, 'I baptize thee, John Bell.'

I gasped. A peculiar expression passed over John Bell's face. I knew what he was thinking. 'Am I supposed to make him my heir, when I can barely support myself?' Mrs Grimsby had informed us that Indians on reservations loved to name their babies after teachers, nurses, and workers. Several of the children had told John that this mother was going to name her baby after him. He had taken it for granted that the baby's name would be 'John' only.

The newly made John Bell opened wide his large, black eyes and stared at Mr King. Then the cold drops splashed on his head, he screwed up his face and let forth a frightening howl. Girls giggled, boys laughed outright. Unselfconscious Mrs Tilliconce padded back to her pew, settled her baby, naked from the waist down, into her comfortable lap, and flopped down the front of her waist. The baby clamped on to the waiting brown nipple, and held on like a leech. Secure from harm, he cuddled against the soft, full breast, tugging to the rhythm of Mr King's droning voice, as he guzzled at the seemingly endless stream of warm, nourishing milk, with toes wiggling.

The next baby to be baptized was a frail, dying mite. Her

mother, Norma Johnston, had to be dismissed from the School with tuberculosis. Later she had married Paul Thomas, an athletic School graduate, and when her baby girl was born, she died. Paul, who had broken out in a mass of running sores, for which Dr Provost could not find a cure, was not able to care for his daughter. So he gave her to his mother who could not or would not speak or understand English.

The previous nurse had tried to save this pitiful baby. When I arrived on the scene, the baby's body, a mere skeleton, was a constant source of infection in the village.

Mr King had brought several of the older pupils into the home, to impress into the children's minds the necessity of Christian baptism. Tillie rocked back and forth crooning to the baby. Skookum George, the grandfather, sprawled out on a cedar mat on the floor behind the kitchen stove, greeted us with his customary grunt, then continued to talk to Big John in their own language. Their mask-like faces gave me the impression that neither of them appeared to notice, or care, what was going on about them. However, I had learned that impassive or blank faces and indifferent attention, did not indicate disinterest. These old and young Indians even when keenly interested could assume the camouflage of indifference whenever they wished to do so. Later they could give minute details of what took place. I learned to assume the same indifferent attitude when occasion warranted.

Ellen took one look at the skeleton baby, wiped a tear from her eyes, and whispered, 'I never saw anything so pitiful.'

The children stood around the room. Paul Thomas, on the kitchen couch, was resigned to pain. Tillie lifted the baby, too sick to notice the change, from the crude, homemade cradle. Mr King took the baby in his arms, and pronounced, 'In the name of the Father, the Son, and the Holy Ghost, I baptize thee, Elsie.'

I was thankful that he omitted the clause, 'Bring up the child in the nurture of the Lord.' Such a clause would have been mockery. It was evident that this little soul would soon be resting safely in the arms of her Maker.

Stoical Tillie said, 'Tanks for making Elsie Christian.' It was a long sentence for Tillie, who always shrugged her shoulders, and muttered, 'I no understand.' A pleased expression passed over Paul Thomas' face.

When Joe Frank, the father of the next baby to be baptized, asked Mr King to baptize their daughter, he said, 'I am Protestant and Matilda is Catholic. She not yet say "Yes". She may hide the baby after service.'

Matilda had stopped preparing dinner, and sat nursing her baby, clad in a one-piece dress. The child, cuddled on her mother's lap, was wiggling her toes and making satisfied, sucking noises. Unselfconsciously Matilda sat in her grubby apron until Mr King came to the place in the service where he had to take the baby into his arms. The baby refused to leave the loosely hanging breast, clasped her vice-like gums on to the nipple, hung on to the bitter end and gave up only when the stretched-out nipple snapped back into its normal position.

Joe took a piece of cloth, no doubt the family hand and dish towel, from the clothes line above our heads and tucked it under the baby's damp, bare bottom. This full-blooded Indian girl, with a mass of long straight black hair, cooed and kicked while Mr King read, 'I baptize thee, Milly.'

Because of the regulations about schooling, I was surprised to discover Rachel, Milly's eight year old sister at home; not in any School. Gladys explained, 'Her mother wants her to go to the Catholic School; the agent, priest, and Mr King cannot agree who should have her.'

When Mr King confirmed Gladys' statement, John remarked, 'I wonder if Milly will be also a pawn between different religious beliefs? If so they had better start their bickering now so that she may get into some school when she is six years old.'

Mr King raised his eyebrows, gave John a glance, opened his lips, but closed them without making any remarks. I knew now why an Indian lawyer had said that disunity in churches competing to chop up reservations into inter-denominational territories was detrimental, and that if Christianity had a message that was good for Indians, denominations should unite.

Tillie and Paul Thomas, who had professed their faith in the Christian religion, seemed happy that Mr King had baptized Elsie. However, it was hard to make them understand that a

death certificate is required before any dead person can be
buried.

The following morning, I heard old women wailing loudly,
and found Elsie's cradle empty. Paul Thomas knew that he
should have notified Mr King or me when Elsie died. He also
knew that relatives of Christians usually had a minister or lay
person say a few religious words at a funeral, and I suspected
that Tillie understood more than she would admit.

It was my duty to investigate such an irregularity. I questioned
Paul, but he merely shrugged his shoulders, pointed to his
mother, and said, 'She thought I had suffered so much she did
not waken me.'

Tillie's face assumed that absolute, blank expression, so common to Indians when they do not want to understand government ways. Other Indians evaded my questions, or said that
Elsie had died a natural death. Chiefs Atlon and Kenderson
were away from the reservation, and Chief Swan, through an
interpreter, said, 'I no hear until morning.'

I was suspicious about the evasive answers regarding a natural
death and a quick burial, so I reported my findings to Mr King.
He was substituting for an ordained minister, and it was his
duty to make out all death certificates. He knew Indians and
their customs as well as legal requirements better than I did.
He shrugged his shoulders, and replied, 'It's not my responsibility.'

I had no authority to act on this side of Canadian law, and
could not go over Mr King's head. The police never acted. They
no doubt worked on the theory that the offenders, with no
money to pay a fine, would have to go to jail, thus involving
considerable public expenses. I discussed the situation with the
teachers, and we agreed that it would be senseless to dig up this
tubercular infected body for an autopsy. I had no authority to
order an autopsy. The wee mite had suffered practically every
moment of her short life, and had been a constant source of
infection for adults and children. She was better left to rest in
peace. I stopped going round in circles, and entered the death in
my ledger. 'Elsie Thomas last seen yesterday in dying condition.
Missing today. Father states she is dead and buried.' I had done
my duty and had a clear conscience. Nevertheless, I did give the

Indians a threatening warning that I would report anyone who buried another body without the proper death certificate.

Lack of accurate death certificates makes Indian statistics inaccurate. I am informed that for some peculiar, unknown reason, many supposed-to-be-dying Indians, especially babies and small children, have been whisked away to other reservations, where there were no doctors or nurses. There, they have been treated by witch doctors and lived to grow up.

I read recently an article, which made me wonder whether perhaps Indians are justified in seeking relief from witch doctors and whisking babies away! This nurse asked for assistance for a sick Indian baby. She was refused this aid by the agent, the only person authorized to act on behalf of the Indians of that reservation. He claimed that the Indian woman's husband was not a member of that particular band, and advised the nurse to get a man to make a box for the baby. The same agent refused to give the nurse permission to buy milk for the baby and charge it to the baby's father, who had credit at the store. In a last attempt to save the baby, the nurse begged to be allowed to take the mother and child into her own home and care for them at her own expense. This request, also, was refused. And, this happened to a helpless, sick baby less than a year old, not in far-off Africa or Asia, but in Christian, democratic Canada.

Any mother who has had to listen to the pathetic wail of a sick, starving baby, in the midst of luxuries, may realize how this mother felt, the effect on her people, on all Indians, and on the nurse. Workers among the Indians will understand the words Senator Gladstone is reported to have said at the annual Pow Wow – that it would be his task to try to recover the lost pride of the Indians. And why, in his maiden speech in the Upper House, 1958, Mr Gladstone told his audience that the Indian people had loved this beautiful country of Canada, and that they want, not the patronage or tolerance of their fellowmen, but understanding and help so that they may materially improve their lot, and achieve equality of opportunity and equal status.

CHAPTER 5

'TAKE NO THOUGHT FOR THE MORROW'

For a week rain had teemed down and high winds swept the Coast. Then hot, depressing humidity clamped down on the village and I had to force myself along the boardwalk. At the third house, Minnie motioned for me to come inside. She held up her arm, exposing an angry infection around a splinter, and made signs that she wanted me to do something about it. An incision would be absolutely necessary, and I was not in the best humour to tackle this ugly, neglected sore. I held up my needle, pointed to the iron pot on the stove, and said, 'Boil water.'

Minnie shrugged her shoulders, pointed outside, and muttered, 'No wood. No fire.'

Her husband, Big John, fully dressed, asleep on his bunk, was not really lazy, he just never had a stick of wood ahead. I made Minnie understand by sign-language, that I would not touch her sore without boiled water. She shook Big John partially awake. He grunted, 'Go later,' turned over to go to sleep. Determined not to make an incision without a sterile needle, I started for the door.

Big John sat upright, opened his eyes, and muttered, 'Too tired. Get driftwood later.'

I was under the impression that neither of them could understand English. Nevertheless, I decided to give them a penny's worth of advice on foresight. I pointed to the stove, and said, 'Always keep wood there and not have to waken when tired.'

Imagine my surprise when John, with a twinkle in his eyes, replied in good English, 'Last Sunday, Mr King read, "Take no thought for the morrow." '

I gave him a piercing look, he grinned sheepishly, and I stalked outside, chuckling to myself, and thought, 'You can't beat an Indian! Those Sunday mask-like faces were camouflage.'

Later, when I returned, Minnie had a kettle of boiling water

45

and there was a pile of driftwood on the floor. She is alive today and ever afterwards John greeted me with a broad grin.

His lack of wood was not a rare case. Poverty did not breed unhappiness on this reservation. When an Indian put his last stick of wood on the fire, someone always gave him more, or the sea belched up driftwood. I could not help but contrast the Indian and white men's standards of living, and wondered which were the happiest people as a whole. Indians considered time free . . . almost as free as the air they breathed. They counted their time by the sun, moon, and seasons. Minutes or hours were beyond their comprehension. Many of the older Indians on Tokawaka reservation could never accustom themselves to coming to meetings by the clock. Time never worried them. They did what they wanted, when they wanted, with what they had on hand.

I came to the conclusion that it takes more than one generation to turn an economic system upside down and inside out overnight.

The following may illustrate the contrast between Indian and white customs better than I can explain them. A game warden met an Indian, whom we will call Simon. He was carrying a rifle in closed season.

'Have you a gun licence, Simon?' asked the warden.

'I don't need one. This is a rifle,' replied Simon.

'But a gun licence means rifles too,' informed the warden.

'Now, how was I to know that the two words were the same? Nobody explained them to me. I always leave my gun at home in off season.'

One little undefined word, 'Rifle', made it illegal for the game warden to enforce his charge. Subtle Simon knew this fact.

About the same time, before the bass season had opened, an enforcement officer met Thomas, an Indian, on a section of the lake. Thomas had two bass in his boat.

'Do you know the season has not opened to keep bass?' accused the enforcement officer.

Thomas with a broad smile answered, 'I am not going to keep them. I caught them for my lunch to eat here.'

Another small, undefined word, 'Keep', made it illegal for the officer to lay a charge. I guess that the warden and the officer had as much difficulty keeping a straight face as I had when Big John said, 'take no thought for the morrow.'

The longer I worked with these Indians, the more I understood (if a person of another race can ever understand the thoughts in an Indian's mind) something of their philosophy of life. Security minus; happiness plus. They lived day by day, moment by moment, and trusted the Great Spirit to keep them, quite a different philosophy to that of the majority of people with whom I had mingled during my lifetime.

I praised Chief Atlon on how well his children Mark and Mary were doing at the School. He replied, 'We, Indians, have had to live by our wits. We may have had a hard life, but it was a free life. If we went wrong, our chief punished us. If we touched another man's wife that was a sin, a great sin, and our chief talked with the wife's husband. Now, with the government away in Ottawa, telling us what to do, we are helpless to act.

I was sceptical about the chief's statements until I read an article which stated that tribal custom was recognized in the acquittal of an Indian youth charged with murdering a friend. He had attempted to lure away his fifteen year old wife. A Court of Queen's Bench jury deliberated less than an hour before freeing the murderer, seventeen years old. The jury said that in reaching this verdict it took into consideration tribal customs, which recognized the girl as his wife, although no Christian marriage had taken place. The reservation where this took place is considered a pagan one. I thought, 'Chief Atlon might not have been telling fairy tales.'

Persons who have never lived in the Indians' environment, under the same economic situations, may find it difficult to understand other facets of their philosophy of life.

For instance, the morning after Norma died, I was surprised, as much as anyone can be surprised at anything in an Indian village, to see two large apple trees, which yielded many baskets of delicious fruit, lying on the ground. Her father, George Johnston, explained, 'They are Norma's.'

I walked along the sandy beach to Norma's grave. There, I saw a small red purse, blue cap, beaded bracelet, two patent leather shoes, and several other trinkets. Tears came into my

47

eyes, when I saw the red vase, containing wild, wilted flowers, dead on their stalks, which a few days before I had carried to Norma, with comforting words from the School girls.

When I returned through the village, I saw her father light a match to a pile of clothing, coat, and mattress. I could not help but wonder where during the past two generations the leadership of this Christian School had gone wrong. With many dying from lack of proper nourishment, fresh food, and improper clothing, supplies of apples and clothing were wantonly wasted when wilfully destroyed. Then I recalled that most Indians had had tuberculosis, and decided that this was the best arrangement for all concerned – especially for health reasons. Fire and sun's rays killed germs. Toys and clothes would not be handled by other people. Although these apple trees provided much needed food, no Indian would consider it wanton waste to cut them down. It was a compulsory part of his religion, like a Catholic repeating his rosary, or a Protestant heaping expensive flowers on a grave.

Mr King confirmed Chief Atlon's statement, and said, 'It is Indian custom. A dead Indian's possession still belongs to him. It must go with him to be used in the next world, or it has to be destroyed.'

When I asked him about a little house decayed almost beyond recognition in the cemetery, he explained that it was a spirit house, the grave of an Indian from another reservation, with different religious beliefs, who died while visiting this reservation. Later I visited an Indian cemetery with many similar spirit houses over dead Indians. And I was informed that these spirit houses were for the dead ones' rights, to be used until all earthly longings were past and the spirit had left this earth to enter the Happy Hunting Grounds. They were built with loving care, shingled on the sides and roofs, with small openings, like those in a bird house, to allow spirits to come and go as they wished. Signs of decay and delapidation are supposed to be evidence that the spirit has fulfilled its earthly task, and has finally departed from this world. Once the houses are completed, Indians do not touch or repair them.

John Bell, who wanted to learn as much as he could about Indian traditions, decided to visit the chiefs the night after the apple trees were burned. When he returned, he said, 'Chiefs Atlon and Swan are no fools. They told me that their chiefs had always tried to keep their people honest. In olden days, they were able to leave food in trees for their next trips. No Indian, unless he were starving, would touch it. If he were starving, he was welcome to it. Today, they cannot leave food and supplies for future trips, because men of other races take their supplies. This makes it hard for their children to understand why they should not do the same thing with articles left outside buildings. Everything placed on an Indian's grave belongs to the dead person. They call it dead man's rights. No Indian will touch anything on a grave.

'Chief Atlon said that Mark had told him that he heard Mrs Grimsby say that Indians are superstitious or afraid of death. "We are not afraid of death, but we do think the evil spirit will avenge us if we do what is wrong. And Mr King says that God will punish his people if they do wrong." '

Regardless of the chief's denial that Indians are not superstitious, I am positive that Indians have a certain amount of fear of the dead though perhaps not more than some of us who say, 'His ghost haunts me.'

We, the Mission staff, found it difficult to understand many Indian customs. Similarly, Chief Swan found our philosophy just as difficult to understand. He could not put his philosophy of life into writing, but he had learned through experience that in many or most cases materialism destroys something in man which submerges his soul, and later leads to rebellion, disobedience, or deception. He and other Indians, by instinct or otherwise, lived their philosophy, always with only bare necessities, but they never coveted or touched the property of another Indian. These Indians (and thousands of others in Canada) lived peculiar lives. Shacks, called homes, were provided for them. Their children were clothed, fed, educated, and trained in the white man's ways – and their whims. Relatives were given a blanket (begrudgingly) to wrap about their dead, and boards to make a box for a grave.

They had no taxes, insurance, light, heat, or school expenses to worry about. Thus they were able to live, day by day, with a more implicit trust in the benevolence of Providence, or their

Great Spirit, than can the average person of a more complex civilization today. With no worry about sickness or death, they had no thought for the morrow. Their philosophy of life made me recall the saying, 'Few people can stand prosperity, but most anyone can adjust to poverty.'

The day sparkled with sunlight. The sky was a beautiful sea-blue. The air was so light it went to my head. Nostalgic memories of summer picnics, lemonade, ice-cream, and home brought a longing to enjoy just one picnic with relatives. I was about to set out for the village when I heard, 'Where's Freddie? I have not seen him since breakfast.'

During Freddie's first weeks in the School he had caused Mrs Grimsby many a headache. Watching for a chance, he could vanish quicker than an eel. The first time he was missing, search parties were combing the campus, beach, woods, and trail, when his father, with Freddie, grinning from ear to ear, sauntered up the boardwalk. After that episode, when someone asked, 'Where's Freddie?' Mrs Grimsby sent one boy scurrying along the beach and another to the village. By the end of the first month Freddie decided to obey, adjusted himself to School routine, and was contented to play about the campus. Nevertheless an occasional desire swept over him to see his mother. He watched his chance and disappeared.

Although he seemed satisfied with School life, he could not conquer this wandering bug. One morning with no thought of the incoming tide he sneaked along the beach. Jimmy found him squatted on a small rock, gazing seaward, the incoming tide creeping up his bare legs. Another day, he was almost asleep on the beach with the tide up to his waist. Still another day he reached home and was having a good time. Each time he returned to the School willingly. When I asked him why he had run away, he grinned, shrugged his shoulders, and replied, 'Saw Mother, Baby knew.'

This special day when I heard whisperings among the boys, I surmised that fifteen year old Jimmy liked to see his mother, thought this a legitimate excuse, and had taken Freddie home for a visit. I had a warm feeling round my heart for the two brothers, tall Jimmy and wee Freddie.

50

This morning, as I walked along the boardwalk, through the bush, I could sympathize with Freddie.

The afternoon brought disruption. It was a Monday and one of those days full of injustices. The peacefulness of the morning walk seemed far away. Tom and Mark, lugging Sammy, came up the walk from the old wharf. They dropped him on to the dispensary cot, and Tom explained, 'He was trying to do a new gymnastic stunt and struck his head on a beam.'

He had not regained consciousness when Wilbur entered carrying a gory-faced Freddie. His arms, legs, and hands were beating a staccato protest, and his shrieks could be heard a quarter of a mile away. As Wilbur plunked him down beside Sammy, he remarked, 'Don't think it is much of a cut.'

Freddie stopped screaming, and sobbed, 'Not hurt, just blood.'

'Why are you screaming?' I asked.

'Miss ports (sports) night', he whimpered.

A Band Aid over the spot brought a grin and 'Tanks'.

Poor Freddie had taken so many blows, cuts and knocks he accepted them as part of life. But eats were his idea of heaven. The thought of his young-robin stomach missing cocoa and cake was too much for him.

The afternoon eventually ended. Physically and mentally fagged, I looked forward to a quiet supper. It was not to be so. Mr King entered, gulped two glasses of soda water, and muttered, 'Soggy food. Not fit to eat.' A sure sign that he, too, had spent a trying day and was in one of his dyspeptic moods. No one dared introduce conversation, thus, supper was eaten quickly, under tense strain.

Nine-thirty eventually came. Over sixty lively children settled for the night. Blessed quietness reigned. John turned the dormitory key, slumped into a chair, and exclaimed, 'No lambs can stray until six in the morning! Thank goodness we can have a quiet peaceful evening.'

A sudden thought struck him, and he said, 'How do you feel about some cool air on a moonlit beach, to get away from the School atmosphere and Indians? This is the first time the three of us have been free for an evening together. Let's not waste a precious moment of this beautiful night and heavenly freedom.'

Our drooping spirits revived. With our bathing suits under our coats, we tiptoed downstairs, raided the kitchen, filled our lunch basket, and sneaked out the back door. As we hurried along the walk, like prowling Tom cats, John whispered, 'Sh-sh, we must not let the villagers hear us.'

Leaving the village behind, we came to the wharf, pushed off in the School punt, and started towards the sulphur spring, half a mile away. The marvellous moonlight, after the swelter-ing day, was a rarity for this time of the year. The creaking of the oars was the only sound in the blue-black night. As we rowed over the silent water, tiny, pearly drops, from the oars, made little tinkling sounds on the water, pushing rippling waves, which gradually widened until they lost themselves shoreward. Moonlight etched geometrical patterns in the heavens.

'What an ideal night for a dip!' exclaimed John.

Ellen, a university graduate, in love, and moon-dreaming, came back to earth, and asked, 'I wonder is it worth spending years battling with these papooses?'

I was too peaceful and too relaxed to do deep thinking, but forced myself to reply, 'I suppose, during the next two genera-tions, some flower may be the fruit of something you or I have said today, as we struggle with the children's problems. These children will be old tomorrow, teaching others what we are teaching them today.'

'Aw, why worry?' exclaimed John. 'On a night like this, let's be young again. See those stars, moon, and sky, that does not require thinking. Civilizations may fall, humans will pass, the world will rush onward and the sky will look down on genera-tion after generation of mere humans for millions of years. No doubt all the time God is struggling with rebellious whites and Indians, trying to teach us to live and not buck nature, just as we are struggling with our papooses day by day.'

My soul soared back into the moonlight. But not for long. The boat bumped the mucky shore, and I was jerked back to earth.

At each step our bare feet squish-squashed, ankle-deep in muck; coming up like drumsticks. The upward suction made them snap like bubble gum.

As if to intensify the thoughts of our anticipated swim, the Aurora Borealis shot out incandescent rays of swiftly, shifting colours. It changed quickly to a celestial, gauze-like sheen, which lit the whole sky.

'I'll beat you to the spring,' said John.

He sprinted ahead, his white legs twinkling in the moonlight. He climbed up the logs, stood ready to dive into the spring, then uttered a dismal wail. 'Can you beat it? Would you believe it? The Indians have chosen this day of all days!'

Twelve year old Bertha, in the School, resented laundry training. She had told us that once a month they bundled their soiled clothing into a wad, rowed across to the sulphur spring, had a social hour, while washing their clothes in the log wash-pen which their men had built around the spring.

John continued, 'Trust the Indians to find a way that requires a minimum amount of labour. Our chemistry teacher told us that sulphur bleaches and disinfects. They can have their clothes white and free from fleas with practically no labour involved.'

I recalled that Bertha had said that the men made a drain hole and plug under the wash-pen. When they finished washing they simply pulled out the plug. And, this afternoon, grease, fleas, and thick water had spewed through the logs into the muck, with its beauty or poison. When I recalled how we had squelched through, my stomach had butterflies on wings.

Clad in dry bathing suits, sitting on our coats, on the cool, dew-damp knoll, thermos of hot cocoa was nectar. By the time we finished our cocoa the sky had darkened and there was a rumble of reverberating thunder, followed by zigzags of lightning.

Pointing to the sky, John said, 'Something seems to tell me that those dark clouds rolling across the moon are an omen for us to start home immediately. But let's chance it! I want more than a whiff of sulphur.'

We sat on in the soft, night air, basking dreamily; words seemed superfluous. Overhead, the moon and rain clouds battled for the right of way. The sky darkened to an eerie ebony. A shivery chill crept into the air, and the wind cut through our suits. When our teeth began to chatter, we gathered up our picnic cups, and John climbed up on to the logs, jumped with a splash, into the sulphur water, and shouted up, 'Only a couple of feet deep, but luxurious. The look of that sky tells me you should get a move on and not wait for more water.'

Ellen and I dropped down beside him. Oblivious to wind and weather, we splashed about until our bodies were delightfully relaxed – tingling and glowing. Puffs of moist air struck our soaked suits and raised goose flesh pimples.

On the way home, never good at directions, I could not see a foot ahead in the inky darkness, and had no idea which way to turn.

'This is your lark, John. It is up to you to get us home,' warned Ellen.

'I'll get you there safe and sound,' he replied, and under his breath, 'I think.'

He slid his hands about in the gooey muck until he felt the faint impressions left by our earlier foot-prints. We wiggled our toes from one print to the next, and crept along behind him. It was midnight before we tied the boat to the wharf and started up the muddy path. As we groped our way, silently, along the trail, through the silent village, rain lathered our faces. Not a dog barked.

When we felt the boardwalk, John cautioned, 'A misstep on these greasy planks will land you stuck headfirst in the black swamp until daylight, because I'm certainly not coming down to dig you out.'

We joined hands, like a string of sausages, and sloshed along. Rain pelted on the planks, filled our ears, and trickled down our necks. Halfway through the woods, we paused to get our breath, shivered, and huddled together. A weird, human-like shriek suddenly rent the air from the thick underbush almost at our feet. Ellen's hair sprouted upright. She grabbed my arm. Quicksilver chills ran up my spine and my goose-flesh body froze.

John, who had heard tales of cougars' eating people alive, exclaimed, 'A cougar, too close for comfort!'

About one o'clock, we straggled into the dark School, chilled to the bone, with our celebrating mood dampened.

Mr King met us, his black hair fairly bristling, and his

moustache twitching, as he exclaimed, 'Idiots. What on earth possessed you to do such an utterly foolish thing? Whoever heard of such a crazy idea?'

Although he berated us, there was an anxious note in his voice, which made us feel rather childish; although we were at liberty to spend our free time as we pleased.

John whispered, 'We may have acted like goats, but it was worth it. No use trying to explain what prompted us.'

I whispered, 'That marvellous sky! The cool dip! The peaceful evening! I would do it again.'

Satisfied, physically tired, and mentally relaxed, we slunk upstairs, like scolded puppies, undressed in the dark (for the generating plant shut off at ten o'clock), and slept like innocent children.

Carefree and feeling on top of the world, I came to the fourth home in the village. There, a strange Indian motioned to me and pointed to my nursing bag. I had learned that these Indians, especially the older ones, loved pills. At sight of my nursing bag, some acute ailment could develop, requiring an immediate pill. I had already come to the conclusion that psychiatrists' theories were correct; theories that mental suggestion can create a sudden desire for pills, treatment, or sympathy, which can develop into a real illness.

The officials of the Department of Indian Affairs had also learned that Tokawaka (and others) Indians had a tendency to hoard certain pills to make home brew. I had been instructed not to give Indians aspirin tablets and certain drugs to take home. There was a fine imposed on anyone selling British Columbia Indians any essence, such as lemon, vanilla, or other extracts, which contain alcohol. This enforcement law was made because old chiefs, who signed treaties, years ago, insisted that an alcohol protection clause be inserted into treaties to protect all Indians from the bad influence of liquor, at that time, being introduced to them by white bootleggers.

This Indian rubbed his hand back and forth across his abdomen, pointed to my bag, and said over and over, 'Stomach ache!' From previous experience, I knew that such a suddenly developed stomach ache would continue, and that he would persist, until I handed him something to swallow. I produced an ever-ready chocolate-coated laxative. These pills were harmless, many times beneficial especially if the person had been gorging on seal meat. I handed him two of these pills. He persistently refused to put them in his mouth. As persistently, I refused to allow him to keep them unless he swallowed them. Eventually, after much motioning, he rolled the pills over in the palm of his hand, and gesticulated something which I could not understand. With a disgusted expression on his face, he tossed the pills into his mouth, gulped once and swallowed. Before those pills could reach his stomach, but too late to retrieve them, young Bill Thomas sauntered along. The two men chatted in Indian, then Bill, with a stoical smile, explained, 'It is his woman who has the stomach ache.'

Nurses on this and other reservations could tell dozens of similar incidents.

Peter had suffered earache for several days. As a trip to the doctor involved three hours, calm water, much longer when rough, it was not undertaken unless for emergencies. I decided that ear trouble, so close to the brain, could be classed an emergency not a case to take a chance.

'What is your trouble?' asked Dr Provost abruptly.

'I had earache all next week,' replied Peter.

'Do you have frequent sore throats?'

Taken by surprise at the direct question. Peter replied, 'Yes, Doctor.'

'Book him for a tonsil operation the next time I visit the School.'

'But, Doctor, I meant, "No". It is my ear not my tonsils,' exclaimed bewildered Peter.

It was never wise to ask any of these Indians a direct question, one which required a complex answer, especially if he had to formulate a statement on the spur of the moment. I intentionally forgot to remind the doctor about Peter's tonsils. He still has them intact and enjoys good health.

The Indian agent and the teachers, also, encountered many humorous situations. John told us once about asking three children, in different grades, to write sentences containing the word 'worms'.

Mary wrote, 'When I gets cold I worms myself.'

Bertha took a different view, and wrote, 'It looks worms outside,' while Peter wrote, 'I hope it worms up this afternoon.'

In another sentence Jimmy wrote, 'We played ball next week and our side won tomorrow.'

A few days before I had seen Jeannie in the hall during class period, and I asked her why she was not in the class room. She replied, 'I get worms.' I coaxed her into the dispensary, but she persisted that she was not sick; still persisting, 'I get worms.' I decided that she was not sick enough for medicine, and let her go back to school. That evening Ellen explained that Jeanie was shivering, so she had sent her across to get warm.

Even the older children found guttural sounds such as warm and worms difficult and perplexing. Due to the fact that the children learned their first English words and sentences in the class rooms, not on the street, they used remarkably good grammar and English. But most of Tokawaka Indians had difficulty distinguishing between today, tomorrow, this week, next week, and several other phrases.

I was informed that these Indians never had any written language. Before most of the little ones entered the School they had picked up scattered words from the older children, but they did not have continuity of thought in their sentence structure. Beginners could not take the regular lessons until they had learned some English.

Not to be outdone, Mr Brant related his recent experience, which might have had a tragic ending. He docked at Kulika, a small fishing cove with three shacks, where the Indians went at certain seasons to fish. No Indians surrounded his boat as they usually did, asking for their slips, so he knew that something extraordinary had happened to distract their attention from these slips. He could hear a murmur of low voices in a nearby home, so he edged himself in between men, women and children crowded about a bed. He recognized Wilfred Signmore in bed, with two of his friends holding his legs. Two others, were holding the ends of a piece of tough kelp (rope-like seaweed). He knew from experience that the moment they thought the end of Wilfred's life was about to come they would taut the ropes. His wife held a plaid scarf ready to throw over her husband's face. With the rope tauted the struggle would be over, and the old woman would start wailing to drive away evil spirits. Although Wilfred seemed to be suffering excrutiating pain and gasping for breath, he was not even moaning, and he did not appear to be afraid to die.

Mr Brant said that he ordered the men to release the kelp. As a shot in the dark, he coaxed Wilfred to swallow some indigestion pills, which he carried with him, for just such emergencies. The pills worked a miracle. In a couple of hours, he was feeling better, and he is alive today to care for his family of six. Later, Mr Brant discovered that a seal blubber feast with gorging the previous night had caused the pain. He said, 'I am positive that this act was motivated by love, not by cruelty. In the absence of medical aid or drugs they were doing what they thought best for a loved one. Most Indians endure pain without fuss, but they cannot bear to see their sick ones whom they believe to be dying suffer severe pain.'

John whispered, 'In spite of his rough exterior, Mr Brant really has a spark of kindness, and gives credit where it is due.'

Most of Tokawaka Indians had faced many hardships, suffered much sickness and faced death many times, yet they were affectionate. Norma's mother held a scarf ready to throw over her child's face before she drew her last breath. When I asked Gladys about this custom, she replied, 'We believe that if an Indian looks on a dead face he will be the next person to die.'

This was a Christian reservation, but the Indians would never look on the face of a dead person. Therefore, after Norma's death, although I always raised the scarf from a dying Indian's face, I was careful not to expose the face to any Indians. I had discovered that deliberate exposure and defiance of their customs only antagonized them and aroused an already hostile attitude. I had learned by experience that confidence was won by love and tact; that compulsion never won a pagan to believe in Christianity.

I was out walking with the girls, one afternoon, when Lucy stopped, grabbed Sheila's arm and ran away from a tiny snake. When I asked her why she was frightened of a little, harmless snake, she replied, 'Oh, but, Nurse, it might change its skin.'

'What if it does?' I asked.

'I don't want to die yet, and Grandmother warned me never to look at a snake changing its skin, because I would be the next person to die.'

The morning Skookum Semond was dying, I was amazed to see his box-coffin beside his bed. He appeared to take it as a matter of fact. Several hours later, neighbours lifted him into box and took it out the window. I learned later that caskets were taken out through windows, instead of doors, since otherwise the living would have to follow the path of the dead.

Like many other men and women these Indians had peculiar ideas of the after-life. They believed that men's ghosts remain on earth after death, while their souls go to another country, possibly up into the clouds. They are uncertain how long it takes the spirit to leave an earthly shell. I realized that like many others they are not too different to many died-in-the-wool orthodox Christians, who speak of going up to heaven; people who believe that God lives only up in the sky and clouds. Some people never think of Him among them on this earth. People who would criticize Indians for burning apple trees, etc, will spend thousands of dollars on a casket, flowers, mourning clothes, or buying their loved ones out of purgatory. Tokawaka Indians would consider such things extravagant, wasteful, senseless frills.

The following incident may better illustrate my point. It came home to me recently, when the little daughter of a friend came home from a Christian Sunday School, and said to her mother, 'Our Sunday School teacher told us that Jesus is with us all the time, is he here?' Her mother, nonplussed, replied, 'Yes, Nancy, I guess He is with us here.'

Nancy looked up into her mother's face and asked, 'Why don't you ask Him in for a drink, sometime?'

One day Ellen and I were walking in the woods near the School, and we noticed several large and small, partially decayed, oblong boxes, covered with green moss, tied with chains and ropes in the limbs of the trees.

Curiosity prompted me to question Gladys. She explained that her grandmother told her that Indians in olden days always put their dead up in trees, because they liked to know the birds, not the worms finally got their loved ones. John remarked,

'Trust an Indian to think of such a strange idea. I would never have thought about a corpse from that angle.'

Mr King informed me that the earth on the rocky ledge was too shallow to hide the bodies from roving cougars and foxes, and the beach did not have sufficient sand and earth to cover box-coffins, and so it was not a satisfactory burying ground, because the shoreline was gradually washing inland. The incoming tide had unearthed two skeletons and boards from badly decayed coffins. Wise old Indians still shake their heads at beach burials, and they insist that a tree is the best burial place.

The Indians thought that the toys and belongings on top of graves, or hung in trees, gave them communion with loved ones. No doubt, similar to some people who persist that, by keeping a lost one's chair in the routine place, he or she is sitting there day by day.

The Tokawaka Indians had an ever-present awareness of death. They faced it, prepared for it, and accepted it as part of life. Elaborate and costly devices to restore a lifelike appearance to the body had no place in what they thought was Christianity and they may be right.

In the nomadic state, it was impossible to wait long in one place for old people to die. Delay would mean no winter supplies or near starvation for the whole tribe. At first, I found it hard to believe true stories. One woman, over which centuries seemed to have passed, forgotten by time, faced the destiny she knew and feared. She did not fear death itself, but the way she would meet it. Old, feeble, useless, she knew she would not be a burden much longer. One beautiful morning, before her tribe broke camp, young braves cast lots, and the drawer of the lot, with a stoical face, picked up the customary axe, took the old woman by the hand, she whimpered softly, and stumbled away with him. The young brave returned alone, and the old women started wailing loudly.

Mr Brant stated that smothering and strangling have played (and still do) a vast role with Indians along some parts of the British Columbia Coast. These Indians' belief in eternity was not too different to the beliefs of many people of other races. Most sincere Christians think that the grave is not the end of life, merely a wayside by the trail. I find it difficult to believe that a powerful master-mind – a Mighty Creator – would take such infinite pains to create the most intricate, marvellous body of an individual, only to have it thrown away into the ground, with no part of that indivdual left. That to me, as to the Indians, is meaningless. I agree with them that the earthly body is a temporary trust to house a soul, like a shell shelters a nut kernel. This shell has no value after the soul leaves it. How the soul fulfils its trust on earth decides, in some respect, its destiny, with reunion with the Power that gave the soul, seems to be their fundamental belief.

I could not help but contrast and compare the simplicity, shall I say, dignity, of taking care of shells of their deceased, with some of our foolish, even morbid, funeral rites. So they must appear to these Indians. No wonder they hesitate to accept all our customs. I can readily understand how they are led to think that our hundred-million-dollars-a-year will beggar their economic system, as well as change their whole attitude to life. The chiefs have no desire to have morticians pussy-foot around their bereaved, to change them from their natural appearance, with powder, rouge, perfume, and lipstick, merely so that they can display to relatives a store-like dummy in an expensive casket with brass handles. They wish to remember their relatives as they last saw them, and dispose of their shell as quickly as possible.

Egyptians worshipped the mummified shell and took little thought for the spirit. Indians provide for the spirit and make provisions to scare away the evil spirits, but discard the shell as useless. It is hard for Anglo-Saxons, who are anxious to make the shell lifelike, or non-lifelike perfection, and thus make themselves believe their relative is merely sleeping, to accept the Indians' religion as having any meaning.

I am well aware that mercy-killing is not Christian, and would lead to great abuses. Yet I was brought face to face with the other side of thinking. A friend of mine, a nurse, said that her mother had cancer. She prayed God that she might be spared being a victim of prolonged suffering by artificial stimulation, merely to satisfy the feelings of relatives, or to test new drugs. Doctors had to live and new drugs had to be tested, but she hoped not on her or her relatives. I recalled the Indians' illegal mercy-killing to save unnecessary, excrutiating pain. Her statement made me reflect. If cancer is introduced to Indians, when there is no doctor, no pain-killing drugs, or hospital available, if it spreads as rapidly as did tuberculosis and venereal diseases introduced to them, much unnecessary, excrutiating suffering will be inflicted on them.

Now that government officials are trying to find the best and quickest means of integrating Indians, the above mentioned facts must be given serious consideration. Too long, Indians have been taught that their own religious philosophy, with their Great Spirit and happy hunting grounds, is pagan and bad. But Christians chanting, 'ashes to ashes', yet pretending that death has not occurred, bewilders more intelligent people than some Indians.

I still suffered from constant interference in my duties from Mr King but I felt sorry for him, caught in this spider's web of trying to satisfy his seniors, suffering mental torture. I tried to picture how I would feel if I had five children to support, and was financially insecure. In an attempt to appease overlord superiors and do what he thought right by the Indians, he had stood the strain better than I would have done.

The full force of his uncertainty was brought home the day he exclaimed, 'If I could do what I think right for the Indians, I would change the whole set-up here. Why should I risk being expelled without financial support for my family merely for the sake of a little exaggeration? I have no alternative. That is what the officials and general public want.'

John exclaimed, 'Do you mean to say that if you wrote the truth officials would ask for your resignation, because you disagreed with them.'

'Wouldn't they! You are new to Indian work. Not my resignation. They would whisk me off to a more isolated reservation with worse conditions. I would not even have an opportunity to explain the true set-up here or elsewhere. Many workers have received such treatment. High-up government officials and church congregations want glowing reports to extract generous contributions. They do not want to hear, or let the public hear, about the other side of the picture – the Indians' ideas.'

I recalled church, magazine and newspaper reports. 'Wonder work done among Indians!' 'Indians have everything given to them.' Such accounts had fascinated me. Now I understood what lay behind them.

John continued, 'But Indians are human beings like us. How do they feel about your reports?' Mr King replied, 'We try to keep church magazines and articles about Indians from the children. As long as we have good reports for their records, these appear to be more important than Indians.'

I had a greater appreciation for Mr King's attempts to help Indians, and more sympathy for his unsettled, mental state of mind. But what a life! Was he justified? Who was I to criticize his methods? I came to the conclusion that under the circumstances, Mr King might accomplish more lasting and more beneficial results for the Indians by his strategy than we would by rebelling. Sooner or later, there was bound to be a set-to or crisis.

Officials were finding it extremely difficult to secure anyone (still do) to act as principal, who could give them the desired reports. Once an appointment was made, they more or less forgot about the situation, unless ideas conflicted with theirs.

Mr King, and the former principal, had managed to wangle their wives to the position of School matron. A less complicated situation for themselves, more complex for the other staff members.

Too many persons had disagreed and had been whisked off to poorer positions in more isolated districts to cool their heels for Mr King to take a chance. Officials were satisfied and accepted him as the one and only person with authority for the whole School.

The subtle chiefs and thinking Indians, without committing themselves to words, intimated their lack of confidence in the principals' abilities to have absolute charge of their children, and they were biding their time.

Time passed. It was almost impossible to get help, advice, or be upheld by my superiors. Discouraged, I would gladly have taken the next boat home. Then, I recalled Abraham

Lincoln's statement. 'As I would not be a slave so I would not be a master.'

I did not want to become a master. But, to be a helper in the existing set-up I would have to be a master or a slave. When I heard the children singing with gusto the popular song, 'Don't fence me in' or 'Give me a home, where the buffalo roam, where the deer and the antelope play,' it had more meaning.

Gradually I came to an understanding with Mr King and I was left alone in charge of the dispensary.

CHAPTER 6

'SEE YOU IN FIFTY YEARS'

'Do you notice anything peculiar about the authorities here?' asked John. 'They act as though an invisible cloud hung over them, as though some secret fear was behind all their actions. Or am I imagining things?'

I was greatly relieved that someone else had noticed this disconcerting, distrustful atmosphere.

Ellen, a keen observer, replied, 'There is certainly something rotten in the set up here. However, I don't believe that the officials of the Department of Indian Affairs, Board of Education, and other church organizations, which engage us to these positions are unaware of the situation. The atmosphere here can't be blamed on the individuals, but on these organizations who represent them in the School. I am positive the Kings want to help the Indians.'

John thought a while before replying, 'Tokawaka gives the Kings security and a good standard of living. From what he says, they were practically destitute when they arrived here. So they did not dare oppose any of the officials, even though they had to resort to underhand means to please them. The agent and the doctor seem to be in the same predicament.

I tried to sympathize with the Kings' determination to keep family and soul together, even though it involved hypocrisy. Between alternately pitying and despising their motives I began to wonder if the time would come when I would stoop to the same tactics.

It soon became evident why Indians had mistrust in the School and its leaders. Indians looked up to their chiefs as their leaders, advisers, for religious instruction, and as their government officials – all closely associated. They could see through a bluff.

Before coming in contact with Christian teaching, their religion centred around one Great Spirit and the elements of nature; sun, wind, rain, lightning, and fire, which regulated their lives. The type of religious-leadership at the School puzzled them, and upset their philosophy of life. It was difficult for them, especially the older people, to accept new beliefs taught by ministers, teachers, and matrons, beliefs which were professed by traders, store-keepers, and fishermen, all calling themselves Christians, yet, many of them living anything but Christian lives. Receptive Indian minds cannot be deceived. The villagers and School children heard staff members and leaders bickering and disagreeing in their teaching and living principles. It seemed to them that the most sinful men were endowed with the greatest worldly goods. They found it difficult to know which type of white to emulate.

Tokawaka Indians knew their ancestors had a form of government long before the white man came to North America. Later this form of government became the envy of scholars. One chief remarked that his people ran a workable democracy which was reaching an ideal state. These Indians as a race had much to be proud of. They were trying to obey the teachings of their Creator, who gave them their form of government, and told them to conserve the animal and bird life and gave them the right to breathe the fresh, clean air, and drink the pure water. These primitive folks could not jump from the Stone Age, overnight, and be able to contend with the world gone crazy with speed cars, boats, planes, space ships, etc. Ill-prepared for such a sudden change, too often thrust into a completely different social, educational, and practical environment, they were victims of the worst features of the white men's modern society.

Indians had to accept a government that sent them to jail when they drank moonshine, made and sold to them by whites who went their way unmolested. Especially, after the same government signed a treaty with their chiefs that no alcohol would be made, sold, or consumed on their reservations. Would I accept it without contesting my rights?

Naturally these Indians, as every individual, have the right to choose between good and evil, right and wrong, and must follow their consciences. But when temptation is put before them by the same race that sends Indians to jail if intoxicated, what can one expect?

John and Ellen, struggling to keep their pupils up to date in class work, were discouraged and disgusted as John said, 'With the present set up, how can the Board of Education expect any teacher to compare the standards of Indian children's term work with that of other Canadian children? Beginners learning another language; older children working half time on the campus; all deprived of the home influence and parental affection, which I find is such an encouragement to any child to do his best at home or at school. The senior boys' hearts are out with their parents fishing and sealing – more sensible, to them, than to try to learn latin and algebra.'

Ellen replied, 'Each day, it is brought home to me that living in two places is not good for any children. Only this morning, Blanche said, "When we go home we do not have to live as we do at the School. We do what our chief tells us to do." '

I wondered what the chief told them about our government and our School. That night, when Chief Atlon came for his children, I had a talk with him. He seemed very intelligent and appeared to appreciate the benefits the children received while they were in the School. He said that he was pleased that his children would be able to read and figure. That they would not be exploited as badly as his parents had been. On the other hand, he would like to keep his children with him. It was hard for his old father (Chief Swan), to knuckle to other masters. He had been deceived, been forced from free lands, seen treaties broken, and had his traps robbed. He felt cramped in confined quarters. He thought it unjust to be robbed of the pleasure of having his grandchildren about his home. He continued, 'When we tell him that Mr King preaches about love, compassion, truth, honesty and freedom, he gets very worked up, and says things that are not good about the government. You must not hold this against him, because he is an old man. We want what is best for our children.'

Jeannie had rebelled when Stella asked her to wash her hands, and Stella had replied, 'While you live in the School you have to do what they tell you. When you go home you do what Chief Swan tells you. And he wants you to wash your hands and face so that you do not have trouble yet.' I wondered if Jeannie understood what was passing through Stella's mind? And what

67

Stella meant by biding time? Had she heard this expression from her chief? That 'yet' might mean a lot.

Jeannie and Freddie learned quickly that obedience and cheerfulness were compulsory. These School children, under the supervision of a white person every moment accepted, or pretended to accept, everything, willingly. As soon as they left the School would most of them get married and try to put into practice what they had learned at the School? But thrust into the home of parents of grandparents, it would be almost impossible for them to practise what they had been taught. Many of them would relapse to their old ways of living, as had their parents.

When we were discussing the possibilities of the older boys, John remarked, 'I wonder what goes on inside Peter's and Philip's minds who'll be the thinkers for this reservation in a few years? I would give a month's salary to know what the chiefs really think about our government, religion, even about us – well, a week's anyway.'

We were greatly concerned about another dangerous situation. I hated to think what would happen should the building take fire. Five, six, and seven year old children locked in the third floor dormitory of this old wooden building, which had been condemned for several years as a fire trap, could never escape unharmed. However, John was very optimistic. He remarked, 'Don't worry. With all those fat fleas in the floors and cracks, we will sizzle and roast without knowing what is happening to us.' He added, 'Seriously, it is difficult to understand how such a situation exists today. Why should the lives of these innocent children be endangered any more than the lives of the officials' children? Not one of them would allow their children to be locked in this fire-trap attic.'

Then, I recalled what Chief Kenderson had said, 'We have no appeal except through our agent, Mr Brant, who has to appeal to the senior official of the Indian Branch at Ottawa, way across Canada. It takes a long time for those Ottawa men to think and act. What good would it do us to appeal? Before our appeal got to the last person they would forget what we had asked them, and they would have to start all over again.'

I read recently that one School had indeed been burned

down. But this was a blessing in disguise for no lives were lost, and to avoid the expense of rebuilding another residential school the authorities adopted the Day School system. So now the children have the benefits of education but retain their family circles and are brought up in the Indian traditions.

One morning I finished making my rounds in the village early. It was an ideal day, with mild, invigorating air, for this time of the year and I strolled along the sandy beach instead of the boardwalk. The tide was low; gentle waves lapped the shore, and little sandpipers minced about catching flies. High overhead, I could see a bald-headed eagle circled the clouds. It was so quiet and peaceful, all cares and worries were forgotten.

While we were eating dinner, John remarked, 'Ellen and I are going to take our pupils out on the rocks for the afternoon history class. Come along with us.'

The previous night's storm had spent its fury, leaving foam gobs bobbling on the water among the shoals. Squashy, brown kelp weed rocked gently to and fro on the waves.

We strolled over the soft, mossy carpet, climbed the rocky cliffs, high above the shore line, and sat watching the gulls circling overhead. High up there on the cliff, in the peaceful atmosphere the children found it difficult to settle to dry history. John also feeling lazy asked Peter, the dreamer, who loved to tell stories about his people, to tell us a story.

Peter sat for a long time, Indian fashion, then started speaking slowly and carefully.

'My grandfather and my father belonged to the Cree tribe on the prairies. Grandfather told us that when they were taken captive by another tribe they travelled for many moons over water and land.'

This was living history. John, ever alert to add life to his teachings, closed his history text book, winked to Ellen, and urged Peter to continue. Peter gazed seaward, seemingly communing with some unknown spirit, and then asked:

'Do you know how many buffaloes roamed the prairies when grandfather lived there?'

Before anyone could answer, he continued, 'Grandfather says that before the advent of the buffalo hide hunters there were

69

miles and miles of buffaloes. Hundreds more than any Indian could count. Sometimes he could look as far as he could see north, south, east, and west, and that the whole country was covered with what appeared to be a huge, moving, brown blanket.'

John had been born on the Coast, and he knew something about mid-western history. He interrupted Peter, and asked, 'Is this a true story or are you making it up as you go along?'

'Cross my heart, Grandfather saw the buffalo with his own eyes.'

Philip, who seldom spoke unless asked a direct question, interrupted, and said, 'My grandfather was also a Cree, and he told us that trains have had to wait all day to let buffalo herds cross the track. He saw it with his own eyes. The buffalo herds were killed so fast that in ten moons there were practically no buffalo left, and his people were starving. That is why Indians left the prairies and came over the Rockies to get fish to eat. I swear my grandfather told me all this. He said that he would give all the fish in the ocean for one, good, juicy buffalo steak.'

The day's history lesson was on opening the western North American continent. John, curious to learn how much true or legendary Indian history, quite different to that in the text book, these children had absorbed from their ancestors, decided to tap their minds and watch their reactions. He asked, 'If your story is true, Peter, how did all the buffalo die?'

Peter, reluctant to answer, gazed into space before he said, 'Grandfather told us that the buffaloes were their very lives. He said that they made shelter, clothes, moccasins, and beds from their hides. Drums were made from the tough neck skins. The women made needles, and men, weapons from the bones. Dog-sled runners were made from the ribs. The women used the sinews for thread and to tie bundles. They strung teeth for ornaments. The only pots and sacks they had were made from the insides. The stomach linings were made into water buckets. They got something like what you call glue, I forgot what grandfather called it, from the hooves. Spoons and bowls were made from the horns. The meat was their living. Buffalo waste droppings were used for heat and to cook their food.'

Unless an Indian can tell a story in his own roundabout way,

he will shut up tighter than an oyster. If it takes him all day,
it is never wise to interrupt him.

'Grandfather said that Indians killed only what they could
use. They thought the buffalo would last for ever to give them
food. Then other men called hunters came, who liked money
better than they liked Indians and buffaloes. They followed the
herds with their heavy wagons, shooting and killing with huge
guns. Two or three men killed them and three or four skinned.
Grandfather said that one Indian told him that there were a
hundred or more wagons that trailed the buffalo, with boom-
ing guns. For miles the plains were horrible with the smell of
rotting buffalo meat. Even the hungry coyotes were so stuffed
they sniffed the meat, but would not touch it. Some killers sold
the tongues for twenty-five cents each. The hide hunters were so
greedy they sold the hides for thousands of dollars, but they
never thought about the Indians, who were left to starve,
Millions of pounds of buffalo meat, enough to feed thousands
of Indians for years, rotted in the sun. As long as these men got
lots of money they, and the government, did not care if Indians
starved.'

Lest he had said too much, Peter paused to watch the reaction
of his words, and Philip added, 'Grandfather said that is why
Indians and white men started fighting.'

The true story of the treatment of the North American
Indians by the white people, unknown to about ninety per cent
of the population of this continent, is a story of sad tragedy,
exploitation, and barbarism. That is history. Naturally our
school text books do not teach the true story in detail of what
happened to North American natives.

The fate of the buffalo and the North American aborigines
certainly has not been fair or pretty. It is one phase of history
of which we cannot be proud. We owe a lot to the ingenuity of
Indians, yet we can never undo what has been done. Before
listening to Peter's story, which made me see the history of
Indians in a different light, it was just another history subject.

The disappearance of the buffalo had meant that Indians
had to cross the Rockies for food. A proud, self-supporting race
reduced to near starvation and poverty, had to leave their home-
land, and learn an entirely new trade – make a living by fishing.

71

As fishing and hunting dwindled food became scarce. Pushed back on to unproductive reservations, in spite of their squalor, Tokawaka Indians still hoped for better times. The past was written indelibly in their minds, tales have been told to the younger generations, who now watch the advancement of other races, and are demanding their rightful place in the life of the country.

John remarked, 'It is tragic how quickly such a proud race has been reduced to such utter dependency on government dole. If we like them had watched our living disappear, been defeated, faced starvation, pushed on reservations with harrowed horizons, what would we have done? More unlikely things may happen to our civilization during the next one or two hundred years. We may be pushed back by some advancing nation, and how will we act? Will we say like Frank Thomas, "I can do without a lot, and live on a little. But did you ever lie awake at night and have to listen to the pitiful whine of a starving, innocent baby in the land of plenty? I have, and sometimes the law does not mean anything to me." '

That night, before sleep came, my mind kept flashing back to my trip across the prairies, *en route* to Tokawaka. I recalled the rat-like gophers standing bodkin-like beside holes in the sand. With the approach of the train, their noses twitched, and they disappeared into their holes. I recalled how the train sped past miles of golden grain heads, heavy with life-giving flour. Gold for the west, luxuries for westerners, life and hope for hundreds of New Canadians, food, clothing, and homes for prairie people, bread for starving Europeans, but at what a cost to the natives living in conditions as we now saw them on this, and other reservations.

The fascinating prairie scene took on a different meaning. How helpless Indians must have felt when they saw all that vast land slipping from them. How they must have felt when compelled to yield everything they loved to the white man. How they must have rebelled against being forced to sign treaties.

I recalled the thrill passengers and I had experienced when the train snaked its way through hair-pin curves up the side of the Rockies; then, rushed in and out of black, mysterious tunnels. How terrified Indians must have been when the first, horrible monster – iron buffalo – came racing along the steel tracks across the prairie, up the mountain side, then dived into the bowels of the mountain – all Indian country. I could picture them still hoping to see again mountain goats on rugged cliffs, moose in the green valleys, buffaloes roaming the vast prairie, and fish leaping in rushing streams at the bottom of gorges.

They must have loved this scenery, with its limitless horizons. Then, shackelled, shamed, and humbled, they were herded to government reservations.

Some people state that Indians are lazy, immoral, non-social, and unambitious. I did not see them so. If there are cases, and no doubt there are a few, they are the result of exploitation on the part of the white people. Indians are quick to imitate what a person does. The white man has done a lot to spoil the Indians. How would we feel when we heard, 'The only good injun is a dead one?' 'Those Red Indians!' 'Those savages!' How would we act when treaties were broken?

John said, 'When I looked about those barn-like shacks on the reservation, provided by the government, I wondered why several of the more ambitious Indians had never improved their own homes. When I mentioned it to Big John, he replied, "If we improve our homes, the government will probably take them from us as they have taken our children and everything else, so what's the use?" '

When we were discussing how the government allowed six year old children to be locked in the dormitory of a School, which had been condemned for years a fire hazard; how the government officials apparently considered cod liver oil a cheaper way of maintaining the health of the children than to provide them with decent, living conditions, we decided Big John was right.

Shiftlessness, indolence, and inertia on Tokawaka reservation (and on other reservations) were due to lack of energy-producing food, such as buffalo meat, venison, caribou, fish, seal, and other foods, which kept their ancestors healthy and full of energy. Also, with no goal for which to strive, there is no incentive. Indians are really not as much to blame for their inertia and for the existing conditions, as are those who herded them on to reservations without adequate facilities.

73

Big John's remark came home to me when I read an article telling about an old Indian gazing on the city. He was chuckling to himself, as he remarked, 'White man take our lands from us. Grow tobacco. Smoke himself to death in lungs. Soon, our children take back our lands, much improved, without us doing hard work.' This may be all too true. As Chief David Benedict said to a government committee once : 'To be considered progressive we must exercise the vote and drink more whisky. No thanks ! We'll see you in fifty years.'

Anglo-Saxons try to forget that individual rights were gained by pioneer ancestors fighting, even scalping and getting bounties on scalps. With some knowledge of the North American Indians' historical background one can better understand why it is impossible for them to comprehend such ruthless destruction of valuable food. Why they protested when government officials made no attempt to stop the slaughter of animals on which their existence depended. Why year after year the old Indians have carried their history in memory, told it to their children and grandchildren, until in 1965, repercussions are coming from Tokawaka and other Indians.

These aborigines have left an imprint on the North American continent. They have added colourfulness to it. They do not intend to lose, or forget, their contributions. Conflicts between old and new customs are awakening a young generation, many of whom do not intend to lose their culture, nor to integrate completely with the white race. Putting city clothes and high heeled shoes on a country girl does not change her character. You have to change her thinking. We can only assist individual Indians by helping them to retain their self-respect, and allow them to feel that they are worthwhile citizens, playing their part in this great country.

CHAPTER 7

THE POTLATCH

Potlatches – those bones of contention between School principals the government and the Indians. Accidentally I found myself mixed up with one, and when I realised what was taking place I decided it was a first-class opportunity to better my knowledge of Indian customs and traditions.

Perhaps now they present to the Indians merely an opportunity for social feasting and meeting people from other reservations, and also economic advantages coming from the exchange of goods.

Originally however, and perhaps even now to some extent, the potlatch had a deep ceremonial significance, though this varied from area to area. Mostly, however, including the area in which Tokawaka was in its basic function was to provide an occasion on which people could formally be presented to claim their rank in the tribes. The chief would present his son, or in tribes where age counted as most important his younger brother, as his heir presumptive. Indians were not strictly speaking by birth automatically born to rank within the tribe. They would attain to it, when evidence of lineage and claims to a title were presented to 'outsiders' and accepted by them. The whole Indian system of rank of the traditional rights to use certain crests was very complex. Guests, invited from other tribes, were brought in to observe the proceedings and in return were given valuable gifts. The courtesy would be returned in due course.

There were other reasons for potlatches – in the north to mourn a chief, in other tribes to wipe out some dishonour of the chiefs.

A development of the potlatch that the government naturally enough took exception to was the competitive potlatch. In order to display his power and riches, one chief would invite another tribe and its chief and give away much valuable property or even destroy it by burning it. The visiting chief would then hold a potlatch and give away or destroy even more. This went on and on until periodically some tribe gave away nearly all it owned.

The need to display power may have gone but still the principle remains of giving away more and more. But with the coming of white man who has brought foreign goods into the reservations money payments are required, with the result that many Indians are getting into debt.

Although Mr King and Mr Brant's explanations led me to believe that the Canadian government had passed a law making these feasts illegal, I cannot find any legal restrictions on pot-latches. I do not believe there is a ban on them, because recently one was held in Thunderbird Park, British Columbia, in honour of Mungo Martin and his son. They had completed a big wooden house in the authentic Indian style. The government did not object when he and his son, almost the last of the expert totem pole carvers on the Pacific Coast, held this potlatch, for the chiefs and notables of several tribes.

Tokawaka women excelled in basket weaving, but they did not have reeds for weaving, herbs, or plants for dyeing, and no money to buy the necessary supplies. Women on other reserva-tions had reeds and herbs but no baskets. Thus a potlatch festival provided the necessary articles, entertainment, relaxation, and exchange of baskets and materials without involving money.

After working all summer on smelly stages, splitting and clean-ing fish, and sloshing about in icy water and mud, men and women needed emotional and physical release. Periodic pot-latches provided the necessary emotional and physical outlet. They created an inner state of happiness, more than did a wed-ding. Like a house warming, they gave Indians a break from routine work.

At this potlatch I saw old and young Indians, spontaneously relaxed, happy, and emotionally satisfied, squatted, carefree, about Chief Swan's big room. It was a picture of undiluted happiness. Eyes sparkling, they were oblivious to what was going on in the outside world. Their minds, like minds of naughty children, told them that they were breaking the law of the country, but for the moment they did not care what might befall them the next hour. This moment of bliss was theirs to enjoy to the full. They would willingly take the consequence. I got an insight into their system of playing, then slipped away. From experience, I knew that when the last article had changed hands, they would curl up on the floor. There, utterly exhausted, but relaxed, they would huddle together, forget their cares, without a prick of conscience, and sleep like innocent babies. Then they would waken at seven o'clock in the morning, or at two in the afternoon, still in their clothes, stretch, eat a meagre meal of dried clams, seal, fish, or bannock, drink strong tea, and continue work where they had left off before the potlatch started.

Although potlatches were a bone of contention between the School principal and the Indians, I had not been authorized to report them. The police knew they were being held. They avoided a clash with Indians by simply looking the other way – so to speak. Without the police or government to back me, I felt justified in not interfering with their potlatches.

For a month apparently Tokawaka hostesses had been unobtrusively preparing for a potlatch. They produced their wares from most unsuspected, hidden places, and exhibited them in the centre of Chief Swan's big room.

This particular Saturday noon, when I left the village, there was no sign of excitement on the stoical face of a single Indian. Yet, everyone knew that there would be a potlatch that afternoon. When the parents took their children home for several hours as customary, they knew that the whole population from another reservation would soon arrive. The older children no doubt knew what was going on before they left the School. They must have been bursting with excitement, yet not one of them breathed a word about the event.

Later I could picture the care-free children enjoying every moment, squatting or crawling over the floor. When the parents brought them back to the School in the evening, not one mask-like face betrayed the secret. It would be much better for these children to be able to talk openly about their anticipated parties.

Each Saturday night, as customary, when the children returned from their homes, older girls, under the supervision of a matron, finecombed every head; as a precautionary measure.

This Saturday night, the children lined up to be combed. Freddie slid into the chair, bent his head over a spreadout paper on the floor, and lisped, 'Me first.' Sammy, Bobby, and Frankie, eager and expectant, with shining eyes, crowded close to Martha, while she finecombed every inch of Freddie's hair.

'Not one!' shouted Bobby, in a disgusted voice.

Freddie, a pathetic figure, slipped out of his chair.

'Next,' called Martha.

Bobby slipped into the chair and the boys mulled closer.

Two hoppers landed on the paper, almost simulatneously.

'Two for you!' shouted Freddie.

When mischievous Sammy got into the chair, excitement reached a peak. Hoppers landed on the paper as fast as kernels in a corn-popper explode.

The boys bunched closer to Martha.

'Fifteen, twenty, thirty,' shouted Bobby.

Freddie snuggled close to Sammy, the hero of the evening, and whispered something. Sammy scowled, and replied, 'You can't speak Indian here.'

Freddie lisped, 'Just said, "ope me next time.'"

When each child, with a hopeful expression, took his place in the chair, reliable, stoical Martha's face gave no indication of anything unusual. But I had a suspicion what had caused all the hoppers.

School rules required that any boy returning from home with more than thirty crawlers had to have his hair cropped. During the summer these boys lived like fish in the salt water and they hated to comb their hair.

Simple yet subtle papooses, as most small children, could outwit the more intelligent staff members.

The day after the fine-combing party, ten boys had their heads shorn. Later Peter, with a twinkle in his eyes, said to John, 'There was a potlatch in the village. We knew that several boys from one family visiting us had hoppers, so we gave him marbles in exchange for hoppers. We wanted our hair cut.'

Another day I walked into a home where a gambling game, La Halle, also a thorn in the flesh for the principal and agent, was being played by two men. Although I realized that they were gambling, it was much later, before I learned the name and principles of the game. La Halle is usually played by two teams.

That morning, Joe and Noah were squatting on the floor in the centre of the room, surrounded by eager, excited men and women. Their hands moved too quickly for me to see all the movements; nevertheless I noticed Noah thrust forward his right hand, which held a small stone. He passed it quickly in front of Joe and as quickly, placed both hands inside a sort of expensive apron, or robe. Before I could think, his hand, containing the stone, came out of the apron and he shoved it swiftly under his squatting buttocks. Following a shuffling motion in his apron, behind his back, he thrust his clenched fist in full view of the audience. Joe, his opponent, wearing a similar apron, had to indicate in a second or two where the stone was located. In his hand, under his buttocks, behind his back, or under his apron. A correct guess would reverse the game, with Joe the Player and Noah the Guesser. He did not guess correctly.

La Halle, a simple game of game of chance, does not require much mental intelligence, but it does develop quick thinking. It reminded me of one of my childhood games, How Many Birds In The Bush?

I was informed that the odds are three to one against a player, and that he may lose everything he owns. Fortunately the players are not out to make money, but to test their skill. They play more for the sporting chance than for material gains, and usually they continue until the loser wins back all he has lost. The speed of the player develops a remarkable quickness of eyes. If Indians are going to survive in their struggle with wild life and a battering civilisation this speed is absolutely necessary.

One day Ellen and I were strolling through the wood near the School. We came out into a four by six foot clearing, and faced three weird, human skulls, smooth as sea-polished stones, which protruded from weather-worn, bony eye sockets, nostrils, and ears. The grass all around the skulls had been trampled into hard-beaten ground. A well-worn, narrow path, almost hidden by underbrush, led to the reservation. This was obviously a much used, secret spot, equipped for some purpose, where the Indians came frequently. It reminded me of the wayside shrines in the province of Quebec. Curiosity prompted me to question Gladys. She assumed her typical dumb expression. Peter looked blank, but a surprised, frightened expression flitted across his face. This intensified my curiosity. I intended to persist until I discovered the objective of the sanctuary of skulls, and why Gladys and Peter were frightened, yet professed ignorance of their existence. I hoped to surprise Peter into revealing the secret; if one can ever surprise an Indian. But I did not have to for Peter came into the dispensary, and said, 'My ear ached all night.'

While I was examining his ear, he remarked, 'Nurse, I came to tell you about those skulls in the woods. They are not white men's skulls. They are the skulls of three lucky La Halle players. Before our men start a game, they go to them and ask their spirits to make them lucky in their games.'

John said later, 'Peter must have decided that by refusing to answer your questions you might be suspicious and think the skulls belong to some former School workers. He figured the penalty would be less for him and his people if he told you. Was there anything wrong with his ear?'

'No,' I replied.

A mysterious, benevolent Providence, or nature, seemed to care for these primitive people. By the time a papoose was two years old he required little care. In other words, he paddled his own canoe without upsetting it, and expected only the meagre comforts that life afforded him. He could fall asleep strapped to boards propped against the wall, and waken long afterwards in the same position. Tightly rolled in blankets, he survived the choking smoke in a closed tent or under canvas on a boat. When dipped into icy water, he barely shivered. Paddling about in the rain kept them happy and healthy. Freddie was most happy when he had mud and grime on his face and hands. Confined between four walls, longing to be back in the outdoors, Indians felt shut in. Many of them developed frequent colds and tuberculosis.

Indians never considered a closed door privacy. Freddie went wherever, and whenever, he pleased. Pre-school age children lived intimately close with their parents and grandparents, following them about, doing whatever they did, learning skills and imitating them. They learned much that later helped them adjust themselves to life. They did not realize that they were learning, because their games were a form of practice, mimicking their parents.

Before the advent of the School, an Indian boy by the time he was fourteen or fifteen years old, or even younger, was capable of looking after himself. Indians, in their state of happiness and misery, found that self-reliance was absolutely necessary. Violent death and wanton starvation at times stalked hand in hand with ancestors of these Tokawaka Indians. Such a life granted few luxuries and tolerated few liberties, if they were to survive. But the self-reliant life did develop forcible, rigid discipline along certain lines. This was a powerful aid in learning to be independent, rather like jungle animal life discipline. Unfortunately, since the children have been herded into Schools much of this self-reliance is by-passed. This is what chiefs are worried about.

Grandparents and fathers of our School children, supported themselves and their families along the streams, lakes, and ocean shores – some from the prairies and forests. When they were forced into confined, narrow quarters their independent spirits were partly broken, but never really lost. With the introduction into softer living, and when they became dependent on government hand-outs, their secure feeling of self-reliance was greatly undermined, until the Indians on this reservation felt like caged animals.

Compulsory, forced education, routine meals, and living in a white School, no doubt, for their own good, until some better system is invented, has taken the papoose from his natural setting of outdoor life. Except for a few weeks in the summer at the canneries or on the reservation, these boys and girls, throughout the formative periods of their lives, are so regimented that when they leave the School and try to adjust themselves to a part Indian, part white, life, they feel insecure. Dwindling game, scarcity of fish, furs, and seals make it harder for them to earn a decent living. It is a tremendous long jump from School life, with everything provided for them.

After leaving the School, the majority of them are restless

F   81

and unable to settle down, like young men and women discharged from the army, navy, and air force. A two-way pull keeps them from enjoying the same happiness and contentment experienced in their homes, before they entered the Christian School.

I agreed with John when he said, 'I would have kicked over the traces more times then these children have done.'

I so wanted to understand the Indians and their children's reactions from all angles, so I asked Chief Atlon how he felt about having his children taken from him and educated in the School. After a long period of silence, he replied, 'Before we met men of other races, sex instincts were as natural as our appetites, not problems. Such desires are necessary in order to continue our race, but our boys don't like to be confined to dormitories. When our girls come home they want to change everything and make homes like they have been accustomed to at the School. Only last week, Bertha's mother said that she wished they had a home of their own for Bertha to come to when she leaves the School next year. She will never be happy living as we do, but it is Mother's home.'

This is the reason many workers say, 'What is the use of struggling with Indians, because the children soon drift back to their childhood way of living.'

Although I was conscious of many thoughts behind his mask-like face, he was careful not to commit himself regarding the good or bad influence of the School on the children. Many of the young men, after living such a sheltered life, were unable to cope with the precarious and uncomfortable hunting and fishing life, under which they had to live in order to provide a subsistence. Some of them just did not want to get out of the receiving line too quickly, similar to pampered children who have had everything done for them, and who do not make an effort to exert themselves.

With their attitude that the white government took their hunting and fishing ground from them, many of them say, 'Let that government support us.' Wardship seemed to discourage them from taking any initiative. It deprived them of economic resources, upon which their forefathers originally depended for a living. Although better educated in book learning, they were unable to compete with the white men with his modern fishing equipment.

As I listened to Chief Atlon, I realized what confronted parents and children. Treated as a child, restricted from his native way of living, if he leaves the reservation, an Indian loses his franchise. The government and white people soon forget that he exists, except to extract certain taxes, or to look with contempt on his way of living. Chief Atlon knew all these things, and was biding his time.

Chief Atlon was well aware that mixing with other races could not long be ignored. He was worried, as many white people are, about integration causing or bringing much unhappiness and trouble.

The words, prostitute, anti-social beings, unseemly behaviour and birth control, were not known to most Indians. Synthetic morality had not been served up to them in dehydrated essence over radios, by magazines, and over television. Prudery, which shudders at the sight of naked flesh and which considers the female form an infamy, never entered their minds. Emotional ecstasy over self-accusation, repentance, and penitence, because of some miserable little sin, felt by many neurotics, was unknown to Tokawaka Indians. If in need of food they would take an apple, and not consider it a sin. The person from whom he took it could do the same in his need elsewhere. There was no petty thieving in the School.

When a mother picked up her innocent baby, removed his steaming diaper (if any) and placidly nuzzled the bare-bottomed baby at her brown breast, to draw its birthright, which they knew the Good Spirit had provided, it was accepted as a natural part of nature. There were no sly winks or snickers when such an act was performed at a large, mixed gathering. Unfortunately Indian boys and girls of this reservation, coming in contact with other races, are gradually being introduced to this overpious, slightly repulsive thought of mind.

Dr Provost told me that every six year old child had knowledge of sexual matters far beyond what is in the mind of most North American children of that age, before he entered the School. I agreed with Dr Provost, but I do not think it is the perverted type of knowledge. Home for Tokawaka children was a shelter but not a retreat. When two or three families huddled together in one room, every child was familiar with parents' intercourse. So the child accepted this as part of nature; part of his training – his life and he too experimented with this practice.

When I spoke to Johnny's father, he said, 'Johnny is four years old, and it will not do him any harm. He has to learn it sometime.' I did not agree with him, but it did bring home one fact. The hush-hush method, so detrimental to most children, could not be used here. The open method, no doubt, did not drive as many children to seek contorted information elsewhere as does the hush-hush method resorted to by many so-called, pious parents, who silence their child's natural, innocent questions.

As Chief Atlon said, Indians like any other race did have their problems. 'I know that with some Indians, as with any race, sometimes passion spirals into an urgency that is uncontrollable as fire.'

I asked Chief Kenderson if there was any legitimate reason why their girls married so young. He paused for a long time, Indian fashion, as though feeling his way, before making any statement detrimental to the government, before he replied, 'Every man needs a woman. Marriage and raising families hold husbands and wives together as rivets hold metals. Each child binds the mother and father more closely. It is natural for every girl to want to be a mother. We do not allow our girls over twelve years old to leave their homes without their parent or older brother accompanying them. That is why we take them to and from the School. We do however encourage early marriages.'

'What does an Indian marriage involve?' I asked.

He avoided a direct explanation but from his round-about explanation I was led to understand that spontaneous cohabitation by both parties and faithfulness after the act is all that is required of an Indian marriage.

He continued, 'After an Indian marriage the couple live as man and wife. Should there be adultery Chief Swan talks to the man. If he dares continue, drastic punishment, even death, is the penalty. Of course all that is changing since the white man's laws have to be obeyed. As with any race, some of our men do not obey Chief Swan's orders.'

In a case of adultery, chiefs usually consider the man more to blame than the woman. Punishment was meted out accordingly. Indian women, who came in contact with men of other races, were prompted by a feeling of hospitality, their own desires, or were unable to resist temptations of money and other gifts. Their husbands considered it an act of hospitality to loan their wives to white men.

According to Chief Atlon's standards of right and wrong, before the coming of the whites, there was little if any loose living.

Early in their teens, School girls showed marked maturity – full bosoms, heavy eyes, and plump ripeness of lips. Their highest ideal, marriage, was perfectly legitimate and natural. Their conception of marriage meant wait on a husband, bear his children, do the manual work about the house and considerable outside work.

Although Chief Atlon and his neighbour had changed wives and all were on friendly terms, the word divorce was practically unknown. Gladys explained that when Chief Swan made his son Chief Atlon, his wife was not considered suitable to be a queen or princess, so she voluntarily gave up her position to a more suitable woman. Nellie claimed that their wives had not proved suitable mates for their husbands, and so, by mutual consent, they had changed wives and both families had been happy ever since. We call this wife swapping, or separation without legal approval. The Indians considered it a natural adjustment to an unsatisfactory situation.

Since the Christian faith had been accepted by all, except one Indian, on Tokawaka reservation, marriages were becoming complex and bewildering. Grandparents, parents, even children, found it difficult to understand why government officials, or School staff members, thought Indians had committed some terrible sinful act in not having their unions blessed by a licensed minister, or unlicensed layman.

This is one important reason why officials should send persons, whose characters are above suspicion – persons who make some attempt to live as they teach – to work among Indians.

An Indian marriage is considered sufficient unless the contracting parties voluntarily seek a second Christian service. After an Indian marriage, young couples go through the form of Christian marriage from desire of heart, from fear, or for their own material benefit.

Gladys, quick to notice actions of other people, adapted herself readily to new ways introduced by other races. She gave me an eye opener when she informed me that when their women could not bear more children they accepted the fact that they were no longer useful. But, that they did not attempt to keep themselves looking as young as their children. She had visited Victoria, seen tourists on boats, loved to use long words, which she did remarkably well, and which she thought were high sounding. She stated that their women did not have the trouble women of many races had during that period called change of life. I surmised that she was quoting from some magazine she had read while at the School, or from gossip picked up among maids in Victoria.

My curiosity was aroused, so I searched libraries and discussed the question with other workers. Not one of them had come in contact with Indian women who had trouble during this period. The teachers and I came to the conclusion that Indians' placid acceptance of the natural functions of life, contentment with home conditions, minus frustration, saved them from suffering agonies. The fact that they lived near to nature and did not fill their bodies with drugs, may also allow them to enjoy their trying middle life period, without frazzled nerves.

Feeling sorry for Skookum Jacob, I asked John George Jacob why he allowed his mother to live in the old smoke house. He replied, 'Chief Swan said not good to put old people in homes. That it is son's duty to make shelter in his home. Give his mother or grandmother a separate room or building near him. Skookum Jacob, not want to live with us. She want her own place. She happy and that is all I can provide for her.'

The longer I worked with Tokawaka Indians, the more I understood some of the complex problems, which have crept upon them with the sudden introduction of Christian marriages and their inconsistencies. They have seen many hypocritical practices among married couples representing Christianity, quite different to those taught by the original Christians. Mixed Christian-pagan principles confound and discourage them from relinquishing some of their pagan customs, and strengthen their desire to instil native customs into their children.

For the interest of all concerned, Indians need the help of other races, but fundamental changes, which we are forcing on Indians must be spread over a period of time. We cannot telescope the centuries, nineteen hundred years, into twenty years, or expect Indians to live partly as an Indian, partly as the white man lives.

Chief Atlon advised his people to know where they stood, what to expect, and how they will be treated, before they bite and swallow new ideas, and make drastic changes in their ways of living.

CHAPTER 8

EMERGENCY

Midnight. The terrific impact of my first Pacific equinoctial gale wakened me. It roared along the rocky banks. The breakers boomed on the rocks below. Rain and hail lashed the window panes. Each gust of wind, more powerful than the last, shook the building then roared along the shore. Would we be carried out to sea?

The storm also wakened dormant anger in the fleas. By the rays of my flashlight, I chased them up and down my legs and back. Between fleas biting, building rocking, and battering waves, sleep was impossible. Eventually the night ended. Daylight came. The storm's fury had subsided. I heard Stella pleading with Mrs Grimsby to let the girls run along the beach and hunt for shells and other articles washed up by the storm. Chaperoning girls along the beach at six o'clock did not appeal to Mrs Grimsby, but it held fascination for me. I offered to go with the girls.

It was a brisk, fresh morning. The waves still boomed and spewed foam high up on the rocks. The youngsters scurried from cove to cove, searching for treasures. Jeannie was the first to come, shouting, 'Mine, I found one.' She held up her delicate, pink shell, with fascinating curliques. Freddie, toddling along behind her, lisped, 'I's found his.' I had to admire his precious shell – an ugly, smooth, red stone.

With animal-like instinct, Peter never missed anything. He held up a small piece of sea-sanded wood, and shouted, 'Just what I want to carve an eagle.'

But later that morning a wire from Dr Provost disrupted all routine work, 'Can you come and assist with a major operation? Life boat will call for you at ten o'clock.'

As I pulled on woollens, sweater, rubber boots, sou'wester,

and rubber coat, I glanced out the window. Huge mounds of green water rushed shoreward, burst into twenty feet spume on the shore. Never a good sailor, I swallowed a pint of saliva.

The lifeboat came as close to shore as shoals would permit. Knee-deep in icy water I waded out. Two weather-worn, hairy hands reached down, grabbed my wrists, swung me aboard, and our boat headed out into the channel. The men's clothing dripped icy, briny water into the boat.

Mr Brunet, who manned this lifeboat, said, 'Good sailor, eh? What a night! Guess we are in for a rough trip!' His voice was serious, but there was a twinkle in his eyes. Just then, a tremendous, green wave burst about the boat, showering us with a chilly, salty cascade. The boat pitched forward, water hissed under the speeding stern. My face glistening with globules, I wilted and crawled to the edge of the boat, leaned over, heaved my much-needed breakfast to the ever-watching, ever-hungry fishes, and Mr Brunet threw a rubber coat over my shoulders. Too sick to move, I lay there shivering until the sun burst through the grey curtain. The water rolled greasy smooth before us, and the rough channel was left behind.

For the first time, I fully appreciated the saying, 'One does not appreciate the beauty of a rainbow unless it follows a storm.'

Three black geese honking their way through the air, low overhead, brought thoughts of a Christmas, crispy, brown goose dinner. My stomach oozed gastric juice. The waves of the saucy water, now listless, seemingly have lost heart and strength, continued to slop the sides of the boat.

Warmed by the sun's rays, I went out front with the men, no longer seasick. The cold, damp air blew across my face and cheeks, leaving a film of tiny globules on my hair. The challenge of the sea, invigorating ozone, and cheerful spirit of the huge, big-hearted, life-saving crew, as they vied with each other to serve me, were a bulwark of inspiration. Fascinated, I watched each new wave rushing towards our boat, weaken, then gently glide away. The ripples becoming smaller until finally they lost themselves in the distance.

Energetic Norwegians, Swedes, English, and Icelanders, having foreseen the value of a hospital for such an emergency, had given freely of time and labour. The doctor, a good carpenter, inspired by the other men's enthusiasm, had built an operating table. He had attached a wire, which he could manoeuvre to accomplish an acrobatic feat to raise or lower the foot of the table.

High up on the hill, the nurseless hospital served the fisher-folk of that part of the Coast. Early that morning, an Indian woman, had come to the doctor's office. She was in agony, and the storm made it impossible to take her to any hospital down the Coast. Planes were not then in use in this district. Dr Provost knew that delay might be fatal, and he did not wish to undertake an abdominal operation without a nurse's assistance. Mr Strong, the telegraph operator, who had never seen an operation performed, kindly offered to circulate for the doctor. When I arrived, the patient was ready. I scrubbed, laid out the doctor's instruments, got everything ready for him, showed Mr Strong what would be needed, then assisted the doctor with a spinal anaesthetic. The operation was successful. I remained three hours with the patient, then had to return to my work. A local Norwegian girl and a relative of the patient remained at the hospital. Should the Norwegian girl need the doctor, the relative could go for him. Indians, being wards of the government, were entitled to free medical and nursing care. But they could not be trusted to watch operatives and know when to seek the doctor's aid.

As our boat putted leisurely over the star-spangled water, the sky became a mass of effervescing starlight. I arrived at the school, tired and hungry, checked the children, and crawled into bed for a few hours and slept like a hibernating bear.

Later the doctor reported that Mrs Thomas made a splendid recovery.

The next day, John came into the sitting-room, flopped himself into a chair, and exclaimed, 'I thought I came here to teach. But today I had another lesson from Peter. I learned about birch trees. I was teaching about our Canadian forests. The class-room was scorching. It was impossible to work up any enthusiasm from reading our history books. So I asked, "Boys, how would you like to continue our studies out on the rocks?" Their hands shot up, their books were slammed shut, and they were on their way.

'We hiked along the sandy beach until we came to a high rock, overlooking the wood and water, which was an ideal place to see trees from all angles. Peter's eagle eye spotted what looked to me like an insignificant sapling, and he said, "You were telling us about birches. See that tiny tree? You should have my grandfather here. He knows everything about the birch tree. He told me that in olden days they never cut a birch tree to make fires. Birch trees were like the buffaloes. Their very lives depended on them."

' "Why is the birch so important?" I asked.

' "Grandfather said that long, long ago, some evil spirit had a fight with the thunderbirds and hurled a lot of them into the woods. Some of the birds smashed into a big birch tree. Ever since, the triangular marks made by them can be seen in the wood of the birch. He says that we should never harm a birch, because the Great Spirit told his people that the birch would give them food, shelter, clothing, and let them travel the wide waters. The Great Spirit showed them how to make birch bark canoes long before anyone knew how to make canoes and boats.

' "Grandfather said that his people made wigwams, large enough to hold three or four families, from sheets of birch bark. They were light to carry from place to place, and it took only a few minutes when they made camp, to set up these wigwams. To prevent the bark from splitting, they put little sticks at each end."

'Then Philip interrupted Peter, and said, "Grandmother told me that her people put food in dishes, and caught sap in cups, made from birch bark. She said that when it rained hard they put a piece of bark over their shoulders. Sometimes they made skirts from it. That many times the only moccasins they had were made from birch bark. She made mulligan, a sort of tea, from the inner bark, and seasoned it with sweet stuff that drips from trees. In the spring, they stripped long, narrow strips off the tender underbark, which looked like the spaghetti we eat at the School. They ate it alone or in soup made with deer meat."

'Before Philip could say any more, Peter butted in and continued, "Grandmother has a picture in her cedar chest, taken by a missionary. It has a woman holding a baby in a birch bark cradle on her back. And Skookum John has a wooden gun made

91

from birch bark, and grandmother has an old basket woven from the bark, which she said was hundreds of years old." ' (Time means little to Indians. A hundred years is their way of expressing their idea of a long time.)

'Philip spoke again, and said, "My mother has a fancy skirt in her chest, which is older than she can remember. Her great-grandmother had it. It has dozens of pretty patterns on it. She said that she made many skirts by folding bark into three or four folds, then biting the designs on with her front teeth until they were deep and firm all around the skirts. The same, regular pattern is repeated every time the bark is folded. She said that is the way they got their first designs for beading moccasins, rugs, stitching clothes, and for basket work. Even the string she ties around her gunny sack patterns is made from a strip of birch bark." '

'I learned that hundreds of years ago, Indians, who could not read books, used the birch to ride on, to wear, to eat, to live, to keep warm and dry, and for hunting. I began to think that the Indians' Great Spirit wanted them to take care of the birch tree. No wonder they were lethargic in the class room. From now on not all our nature lessons will be taken from our text books.'

Today, hunters make a little trumpet from birch bark, and their hunting call is a deathly imitator of the cow moose. It is so alluring that a bull moose will come within range of gun shot. No doubt the first white hunters learned how to make this trumpet from ancestors of Tokawaka Indians.

Recently, a hunter tried using one of these trumpets. He rolled a strip of bark, one foot by two feet, into a funnel shape; three inches at the mouth and six inches at the end. He stood in the middle of a swamp, raised his horn and shouted in a tone the loudest he could muster, 'Meah-hs-woof!' There was no answer. He called again. The third time he heard two woof, woofs.

An ex-graduate from our School, Nellie, a sincere Christian, volunteered to act as interpreter at the Sunday School for grand-parents, parents, and pre-school age children. Gladys, who had been taught by a missionary's wife, offered to play the rickety organ in the Community House. Grandparents and parents, with leathery faces and shaggy hair; mothers, babies spread-eagled on their backs, with toddlers tightly clutching their skirts, were mulling about the Community House. It was an opportunity for the women to get away from home routine, though I preferred to think that most of them had come eager to hear about God, and to learn more about His teaching.

Sunday School officially opened as soon as Gladys went to the organ and Jake, the janitor, had given the few hymn books to the young men and women who could read English. Having been sung so many times, most of the hymns were familiar to the other people, who hummed in guttural Indian. The louder the singing and humming, the faster the babies sucked, until, one by one, little wiggling legs dropped limply into mothers' laps.

Each Sunday, I told them a Bible story, in simple words, linking it with something connected to their home life. I never knew how much of the story was absorbed, but there never was a more rapt audience. I would pause, frequently, while Nellie interpreted the story, bit by bit, to the anticipating congregation. Her extremely retentive memory and elastic imagination enabled her to retain and translate the story so that they understood its meaning. Indians like stories told slowly.

The teachers and I wondered why Indians, adults and children, invariably chose, as their favourite hymn, 'Faith of Our Fathers.' We decided that it was the tune, not the words, that stirred their emotions. We sang two hymns; our voices blending with the gently lapping waves, then Jennie waded through the scripture lesson. When she finished, Josie shuffled about in front of us, with open palm, watching closely, to see that each person dropped in a penny, which she counted carefully, one by one. With the money tightly clasped in her hand, as though it might run away, she brought the pennies to me. This money was sent to a mission field to people who did not have as many comforts as these people!

Sunday School ended with, 'Suffer Little Children To Come Unto Me.'

It was never a problem to get participators for our School Sunday School. It was a mathematical problem to choose different people each week to take part. I heard Fannie whisper to Josie, 'Wonder if she will choose me next Sunday? I'd like to do something for God.'

As I strolled homeward along the trail, I recalled an article written by a nurse in charge of a city ward, about motherless nurseries, babies drawing cold satisfaction from rubber nipples. There flashed through my mind a mental picture of disinterested baby sitters and negligent mothers trying to satisfy deep emotional desires by playing cards, dancing, bingoes, and cocktail parties. A strange contrast with this Sunday afternoon picture. Indian mothers may have robbed cows, but they cuddled satisfied babies.

A simple people, despised by many races, seeking guidance for daily living, and praising God in such a natural, spontaneous manner. Many city mothers might consider the natural sucking sounds vulgar, and guttural humming ignorance. But the glowing faces and the whole-hearted participation of mothers, as they sang praises to the Creator – Great Spirit – contrasted strangely with elaborately decked, gowned choirs, cushioned pews, richly decorated city churches, and ministers intoning proper ritual. I wondered when church service ritual had lost this simple dignity of spontaneous worship – somewhere along the engrossing line of interpretation.

Gazing skyward and seaward, I could see a mountainside gather of young and old, hanging on the words of their Great Leader, and then on their way homeward singing or humming praises, similar to these Indians. And many of them were fishermen. I knew that it was not ritual, clothing, elegance, or primitive customs, but the sincerity of the spirit of heart that counted. Each must worship in his own way.

No doubt, Jesus chose fishermen to be his disciples because their very craft revealed some of the essential qualities needed in His Kingdom's work. The fishermen, like the Indians, were accustomed to solitudes of life. They were men who communed with God or their Great Spirit. They communed with nature, on the great deep, amid the dark silences of the night, under the clear light of the moon, and in the burning sun's rays. Indians knew the value of quietness. They had learned to watch and wait for success in their calling. They had learned to persevere and refuse to give up when discouraged. I could not help but think that, like the fishermen of old, Indians also had turned many of their failures into stepping stones of new adventures. They also could toil for days, get nothing, and still persist. My thoughts turned to the Jews coming into their own land. Would Indians again rule their original land some day?

The moment dinner and the last chores were finished, the School children's Sunday School started. The children accepted it as much a part of, and as necessary to, their lives as cod liver oil. Many of them accepted it in much the same spirit. These recesses were a treat for the children. When Sunday School was over, weekly restrictions were lowered. Under the supervision of John and the matron, groups of children could read, hike through mysterious bush trails, or explore the ever-changing, sandy beach. During such periods, these children acted more like normal children than they did on weekdays – their natural selves.

Later hiking along the beach, Freddie, too small to keep up with the boys, tagged along behind us. Game as a fighting rooster, he tried to do everything the older children did. I went back to him. His spindly legs just would not carry him today. He stood there with a pathetic expression on his old-man face, and lisped, 'Legs no go, tired, mother always carry.'

Sheila and Lucy made a four-hand chair, and Freddie, with his familiar ear-to-ear grin, rode home like a prince.

I loved small children, but tried not to show favouritism, though I will admit that I may have shown more affection for Jeannie, Freddie, and Beatrice, those love-starved babies.

CHAPTER 9

THE FEAST

In an attempt to raise the standard of living of these Indians, government officials should not perhaps overlook some of their crude medicines and primitive methods of treating the sick.

For instance, Dr Provost advised me to stand by for abnormal maternity cases, but warned me against interfering with Indian deliveries. They seemed to be immune to their own germs, but readily picked up germs introduced by other races. He insisted that a normal delivery by an Indian midwife was usually without infection. Many times Indian mothers had been infected when delivered by a white person.

The mother, or midwife, bites off the cord. Nature provides certain types of moss and reeds, which seem to be germ proof, and the only antiseptic measures needed. Used as a cord dressing, no more infections were encountered than when sterile gauze dressings are applied.

During recent years, modern scientists have made startling discoveries, as a result, modern hospitals are substituting oil, instead of daily water baths. Tokawaka and other Indians, have always oiled their newborn babies.

Today, screaming newspaper headlines broadcast startling new discoveries and diseases caused by serious vitamin deficiency. Indians did not know the words, vitamin deficiency, and few, if any, suffered from diseases caused by vitamin deficiency if they could get the proper amount of fish, berries, bannock and buffalo meat. I never found any record of scurvy among Tokawaka Indians. Magazines and cook books advocate canning and steaming fruit and vegetables instead of boiling them. Indians ate vegetables, wild fruit, herbs, some fish and game, raw, and dried most of these for off-season food.

When I saw them crunching rose haws, my heart flopped. I had been taught from childhood, that rose haws were deadly poison. With a deflated ego, I began to think that nature was a more efficient nurse in providing prophylactic measures than doctors, nurses, and drugs. I had more respect for some of their concoctions, when a scientist stated that he had discovered a new source of protection against many diseases, especially scurvy – vitamin C in rose haws.

Many of their simple, primitive, external, and internal concoctions are well worth considering. Indians split a rabbit, or small seal, down the midline and attached the raw side to the reddened area of an infection or injury. Modern surgeons proclaim that certain fluids pass through the membranes of the human body and advise osmosis for some injuries. The passing of the toxic fluids, or substances, to the flesh of the rabbit, no doubt, reduces infections in the tissues.

Much hue and cry have been made over the discovery of wonder drugs, such as penicillin, streptomycin, and aureomycin. Penicillin and its derivants are coupled with the produce of bread mould and the urine of pregnant mares and humans. For hundreds of years Indians have given sick people pregnant mothers' urine to drink. But these unlettered nomads never knew that the female sex hormone, oestrogen, found in the urine of pregnant mothers and animals, would revolutionize the world in the nineteenth and twentieth centuries, for better or for worse.

Millions of dollars are spent to produce hormones, such as A.C.T.H., which stimulates the cortex of the human adrenal gland to produce the hormone and cortisone, extensively used to treat arthritis. Arthritis and other bone diseases could easily have developed from long exposure to all types of weather, more frequently than they did, no doubt, due to the fact that Indians used indescribable concoctions, disgusting to people of other races, for internal cures. Mixtures made from brains and glands of animals and reptiles prevented much suffering. In some weird way, these primitive people, sensed mystical healing properties in brain and gland tissues. They knew the proportion of the concoctions, but they were not able to put their thoughts into words. It was left for the white man to extend research, describe the process, receive the credit, and reap the reward.

Long before the white man was born Indian medicine men

cured mental patients by using singing, dancing, and certain concoctions as treatment for deranged minds. Today, medical men are using similar treatment under a different name. Many psychiatrists are stressing the beneficial results of quiet music, hypnotism, and other forms of relaxation for mental sickness.

Big John came to the office and asked for Friar's Balsam. When I asked him why he wanted it, he explained, 'When we are working in the woods we do not get the right food and often we get cramps. We boil balsam gum in water and it cures them. Annie has pains in her stomach but I cannot get to the woods to get any gum.'

I learned later, that Indians healed wounds and lacerations by putting balsam gum, which had been boiled in a syrup, into them. And Nellie told me that they made a balsam-pitch concoction, which acted on the body as the white man's dose of soda widely advertised, gulped, and burped by millions.

The medicine man and chiefs knew that something in the flesh of certain fish oils, such as cod, halibut, and other fish, and their products, kept them healthy.

Scientists have discovered that certain elements in cod, turbot, and lawyer fish provide something which prevents malnutrition.

Indians knew that willow bark with its ingredient salicylate contained something that eased body pain. Today aspirin the basis of which is salicylate is widely advertised for everything from toe ache to upset liver. If advertisers thought they could get away with it, no doubt they would broadcast that it would produce a baby.

For hundreds of years, people of other races have shrugged their shoulders at the ridiculous concoctions used by Indian medicine makers. But in their haphazard search for relief from pain, Indians stumbled on to helpful remedies. Research is providing new drugs from the same sources. The sad fact remains that many of the persons directly benefited by these new discoveries adopt a superior attitude towards Indians.

Far be from me to recommend that we use Indian concoctions, but after watching the use of antibiotic drugs, so freely shot into humans, many times as a stab in the dark, for dozens of different diseases, I wonder if like a boomerang there may be harmful repercussions. Perhaps some future race will think 1965 treatment pagan witchcraft – more so than we consider Indians' concoctions witchcraft?

Indians took it for granted that the natural resources and discoveries were put there for human need, not for profit. Then, thrown headlong into a highly commercialized world, they adopt a certain philosophy, accepting illness as they accept bad wind or dirty weather, shrug their shoulders, and know that when it has blown over all will be well again.

Tokawaka Indians, as a race, have not made any sudden and drastic changes. Although they are slowly and steadily progressing forward, many of them still cling to ancient practices, in which they find more security than in some of our modern customs.

By colourful ceremonies, the older Indians tried to briefly recapture some of their old way of life, long vanished, but still stirring in their blood. They hoped to keep their better traditional past alive in their children's memories.

One Saturday, a heavy blanket of peasoup fog enveloped everything. I could not distinguish an object a foot away. The air was raw and depressive. The cold penetrated to the marrow of my bones. A lazy, restlessness pervaded my whole being. I yielded to temptation, took a book, and crawled into bed. The *de luxe* feeling just to stretch my toes and relax under the blanket, seemed too good to be true. Sentimentally peaceful, too quiet and sleepy even to read, I dreamed. Not for long. A loud pounding on the door broke the spell. I crawled out of bed reluctantly, went downstairs, looked through the peep-hole in the door. I was thankfully surprised not to see a person with a tale of woe, or a sick villager needing attention.

Tom Frank greeted me with his familiar grin, and said, 'Chief Swan invites you all to our feast and dance, about six o'clock.'

I dragged John and Ellen out of a slough of despondency, which was slowly sucking them under. An Indian dance, plus a feast, both new to us, would be a fascinating event. Aches and pains would be forgotten, because even the oldest grandmother and the youngest baby would be at that feast.

At five-thirty, blanketed by dense fog, we inched our way

along the boardwalk. Yelps from dogs and the thumping of feet, keeping time to loud, rhythmic throbbing from sticks on skin drums, guided us towards Chief Swan's home. Ordinarily bare of comforts, destitute of luxuries, never really warm, it sheltered three families. Tonight, it was crammed with eager, anticipating, merry makers.

In the centre of the floor, Chief Swan, sitting on a dais speaking to his people all around, saw our arrival, and greeted us with, 'How-do.' Pointing to a bench on the north side of the room, he said, 'Sit.' Three women slid quietly off the bench and squatted on the floor. We took their places. The chief continued talking for another half hour. Although we did not understand the Indian language, the intent expression on each face told us that the Indians were drinking in every word their chief spoke. He apologized, through Chief Atlon, for using their language. During the remainder of the evening, much of the conversation was a conglomeration of Indian and English. Words which could not be translated into English were spoken in their native tongue.

There was a sudden hush, followed by an air of expectancy. All eyes turned to a side door. Chief Atlon, his five year old son, Benson, John Titcomb, his four year old Dixon, Gladys Titcomb, George Thomas, Big John, Jessie Frank, and Jennie leaped to the platform. Colourful feathers, stuck into plaited bands of British Columbia cedar bark circled their heads. Beautifully designed, coloured, beaded, native costumes, with the thunder-bird-whale-canoe legend interwoven in them, were bound at the waist by another plaited cedar bark band. Vivid red and blue paint, daubed on their cheeks and foreheads, gave them a weird appearance. Their physical bodies, developed in their natural, active, outdoor life, were magnificent. No cumbersome obesity hindered their movements. Each limb, suggestive of action and endurance, made me recall Chief Atlon's remark, 'I wish our children could have more outdoor, challenging activities in the School.'

If the historical and traditional Indians' background is to be retained, these small children must be taught Indian dances before they are taken away from their parents at the age of six years. Prince Benson and wee Dixon must have had considerable training in their dance costumes. Pride and satisfaction shone from their eyes. Watching closely every facial expression and every limb gesticulation of their fathers, they mimicked them in perfect rhythm. I could actually feel the proud thrill of those tiny, whirling, brown bodies.

No fast, twang music of violin strings could have mesmerized and fascinated the listeners as did the continuous, throbbing, rhythmic beat of sticks on the skin drums. With movements performed much too quickly to be perceived by the naked eye, each body would plunge down behind; as quickly rear in front. Their still legs and mobile bodies appeared to be three parts rubber and one part iron. It mystified us how they managed to keep aplumb between centripetal and centrifugal force.

Their bodies appeared to be propelled by some intricate mysterious force. Their skin soles lightly touched, then loudly thumped, the uneven plank floors. They whirled, writhed, stamped, howled, bent, and beat time to the music, on and on, in perfect harmony with each one of the group. There was nothing of the sleepy, sensuous, languorous type of dancing often seen in public dance halls.

Damp hair swept back, bodies perspiring, they performed, with seemingly timeless effort, the real art of dancing, which left no cold-mutton spectators. The only sounds heard from the audience were a few mature and seasoned grunts of soul-thrilled satisfaction. Like some dark mysterious wind or spirit, the twanging music, dancing and dull throbs held the crowd mesmerized. The faster they danced the closer edged the rapt crowd, until, with the last whirling, bending body, dancing and drum throbs ceased abruptly.

Satisfaction shone from all eyes. Heavy beads of perspiration dripped from their steaming bodies. As though appealing for praise or disfavour, Benson's and Dixon's eyes scanned their fathers' faces. With beaming faces and sparkling eyes, satisfied that they had done their best, the boys slipped silently back to the bench. Floor planks revibrated under the thumping of men's feet. Rafters re-echoed the applause. Another set of dancers stepped forward on to the platform.

My mind kept reverting to the words of the poem, *Look to the*

Dawn, by the Indian Kalides, written as a salutation to the dawn. It seemed so appropriate for this scene.

> Yesterday is but a dream and tomorrow is only a vision.
> But today well lived makes every yesterday a dream of
> happiness and every tomorrow a vision of hope.

I thought how like the wise old owl who sat on the oak – the more he heard the less he spoke, the less he spoke, the more he heard. Like the owl, these Indians, with their keen observation, silently heard, saw and used their retentive memories to retain picturesque scenes on which to meditate. Later, they will tell it all to their children and grandchildren. One hundred years hence we hope they will be telling about this dance.

Dancing ceased at eleven o'clock, Chief Atlon stepped to his dais, and announced, 'Eats'. Women slipped back and forth, noiselessly, into the black depth of the outer kitchen behind the wood stove. Recent School graduates placed sturdy pieces of corrugated cardboard, or small cedar rugs, on the floor in front of each person. Gladys and Minnie followed, with tubs of thick, white cups.

When each person had a cardboard place mat, everyone except us strolled over to the huge, copper wash boiler on top of the bulging, iron stove, where Gladys was ladling up cups of boiled, black tea. They meandered back, carefully balancing a brimful cup, and took their places on benches or squatting on the floor.

As Indian hospitality required guests to be served, Gladys filled our cups from a jug of brew. Emma placed a slab of bannock and a wedge of apple pie on our makeshift tablecloths. Bannock, substitute for bread, consists of a thick cake made from flour and water, without yeast. Baked in frying pans, it withstood any sort of weather without moulding. Next to codfish and seal, it is the most important food. But apple pies are the result of outside influences!

As soon as all the people had been served, Chief Swan annouced, 'Eat!' Although it was not customary for School workers to eat in Indian homes, we did not wish to offend their hospitality.

102

Although I always enjoyed my food, until that night I had thought of it as a necessity to keep body and mind healthy and fit for work. I had never given much thought to the satisfaction derived from just eating. I was amazed at the gusto and satisfaction displayed by everyone as he attacked the hard bannock and apple pie washed down with enjoyable gulps of lye tea. No expensive steak served in a high class hotel ever gave an individual more satisfaction than did this plain food, eaten with fingers. With much lip-smacking and finger-licking, pie and tea disappeared as if by magic. Not a crumb was left for the snooping, hungry dogs.

A two-year-old, with a huge wad of bannock tightly squeezed in his fist, sucking another fistful of pie, was balanced on his unstable buttocks on the bench. I expected to see his unbalanced equilibrium catastrophically end. I was mistaken. This youngster devoured tremendous quantities of bannock and pie, and those experienced buttocks continued to adhere to the bench like elastoplast.

As I listened to them eating, I recalled Emma's statement. Mature for her age, with a chip on her shoulder, Emma resented Mr King's dictatorship and longed to be free from restrictions. One day she exclaimed, 'Most whites I know are like dogs. They glut, never work too hard, feed on the best food until they get fat, then they ride in cars. I want a husband who goes out fishing.'

Emma had never met people who owned large cars, and she had never been in a city. I wondered if Emma had heard her chiefs express this opinion, or whether she was just 'showing off.'

As I watched the Indians eating their feast, it was evident that they could use their mouths and lips, as well as their ears, feet, eyes, and minds to good purpose, when they wanted to; each in its own place.

Lucky Indians! They were spared the social conventions of balancing a china cup on a slipping serviette or silk skirt lap. They did not have to watch their hostess' first move to learn the proper use of cutlery. Only a magician or an octopus could have elegantly balanced a cup, pie, and bannock, and swatted mosquitoes and fleas. Unspeakable, hot-tongued mosquitoes swarmed through the wide-open windows and doors, fiendish, creatures with insatiable appetites and fire-like needles, bent on enjoying a diet of red blood. They walked up our legs, dropped on our foreheads, buzzed about our necks, and swarmed about our backs and arms.

A fiery dart in an unscratchable spot and away flew the mosquito to eat his tasty titbit, with as much gusto as did the Indians. Apart from these bites, John, enjoying himself immensely, pointed upward, and whispered, 'Hear that ugly buzzing! Watch that one! I wish they detested my white flesh as much as they do Indians' brown skin.'

Allergic to fleas, I knew that a flea half a mile away, could sniff a vulnerable spot, and make a flying leap, like a kangaroo, for that spot. The assembled crowd, the damp air, and hot perspiring bodies were the fleas' heaven, but they did not go near the Indians.

I did not want to scratch to offend the chief, or make any loud smacks. Yet I could not sit still much longer. It was a relief when John suggested, 'Let's go home before dancing starts again. I simply have to have a wholesale scratch.'

In my bedroom, I stripped off my clothing, got a mirror-view of leopard-spotted legs and hips, and started an all night battle with the midget always winning.

CHAPTER 10

CHANGING WORLD

Had government officials used more foresight when compelling Indians to move on to reservations, many detrimental conditions and much sickness might have been avoided. I attempted to follow up the previous nurse's efforts to have the chiefs build more outside privies. I recalled the words of a Chinese on his return from a visit to the United States. When asked what most impressed him, he replied, 'The perpetual and everlasting concentration on elimination and on alimentary problems. The average North American never has time to meditate, let his imagination expand, enjoy life, or see the natural beauties which surround him. His chief objective, all his life, seems to be to rush hither and yon to make more comfortable and more beautiful his surroundings in which to eliminate the unnecessary waste material from his gluttonous alimentary canal.'

I agreed with the Chinese, but I did not agree that the officials had spent much time, if any, considering the sewerage problems of this reservation. Before Indians were herded into the wooden shelters, almost touching each other, the great open spaces were sufficient for them. Nonetheless natural conditions and nature cannot be overlooked. It is a well-known fact, disgusting as it may seem to many people, that human excreta contains much nourishment for the less delicate, intestinal mechanism of their half-starved dogs. In working harmony with the strong decomposing rays of the sun the dogs made human elimination a fairly simple problem. With homes built close together, new and complex problems confront the Indians. They cannot, or will not, understand why the same system is not good enough for the village.

Money misappropriated, or the amount spent for one visit of the agent, would have greatly improved the comforts of the Indians of this reservation. When I started to investigate the

105

sources of colds and other infections I was appalled. There were only three individual privies in the whole village, not provided by the government – but by some of the more progressive men, or shall I say, more modest men, who had attended the School. Before my investigation ended, I wished officials had been more like the Chinese's friends. The unpleasant duty of calling a meeting of the chiefs to discuss the pros and cons of building more outside toilets was thrust upon me. I explained, tactfully, that many of their colds and infections were caused by germs carried into the well water from the surface of the ground. 'What are germs? Never saw one!' exclaimed Chief Swan, through Chief Atlon. The chiefs sat motionless for ten minutes, then I asked, 'Can you afford to build some more privies?'

Another silent ten minutes, and Chief Atlon replied, 'We think.' This was more than I had hoped for at the first meeting. They would go home and meditate, I, to hope. Each day, I looked, in vain, for signs of another building. Then, one morning too rainy for the men to go out fishing, I saw two, new, solidly built toilets near the beach sticking up like sore thumbs. I went to the chiefs and said, 'Thank you for your cooperation.'

Chief Swan grunted, 'Welcome.'

For the time being, the matter was closed.

The teachers and I discussed the government and the Indian problem many times. We could see that the officials had spent a lot of money for the needs of Indians and much of it unwisely. We also knew that equality of living would never be good for any race or country, for it takes all types of persons and standards to develop a character or a country. John voiced our thoughts, when he said, 'Aren't people who feel they are giving generously to Indian work rather like persons who give beautifully wrapped Christmas presents? The receiver, with anticipation, cuts the outside cord. He strips off layers of brown paper, opens up the tissue paper, unties the beautiful ribbon, breaks the pretty seal, opens up the soft cotton, and lifts out a handsome watch, without "It" that makes it tick.'

Indians are provided with material things – the wrappings – clothes, food, shacks, education, ration tickets, boards for a coffin, but their children are taken from them. The government has also made it possible for workers to go among them and teach them to live peacefully with other races. But when officials continue to send workers among them who appear to make little or no effort to live according to the precepts of their teaching, all this sounds rather hypocritical to these Indians.

Workers promote trust, develop co-operation and unity of a coalition only when they practise as well as preach Christian precepts – love, faith, and honesty. And the security of the Indians and white race depends largely on these tenets.

Although I searched library books I could not find any statistical confirmation that tuberculosis and venereal diseases were unknown among Indians until introduced by persons of other races, though most writers mention this as an authentic statement. I shuddered too when I discovered that one pair of houseflies can have 5,598,350,000 descendants in five months, and that the average fly seldom goes more than twenty yards from where it was born. I thought of the millions of flies on Tokawaka reservation.

Dr Provost told me that as long as he had been caring for these Indians practically all the five and six year olds had been venereally infected before they were admitted to the School, and that every home had, or had had, tuberculosis.

Some workers claim that the state of utter inertia, apparently prevalent through the adminstration of the Federal Department of Indian Affairs, or their agents, might be a stumbling block for more zealous official workers with Indians. I agree. Many of them feel it is impossible to do a good job under the existing conditions, and they become apathetic. Many workers, unable to get any support from the agent, police, or government, have given up the attempt to improve conditions in reservations.

The secret of assurance is pride. The wave of degradation brought about by contact with the white man tore the Indians' pride from them.

In olden days, the will-power of the Indian was his security. It was more important to him than his health. He felt a free man, satisfied with a measure of knowledge required for his occupation, needs, and health, and never considered himself a slave. The chief and Indians did not consider a man lazy because he did not replenish his wood supply until he put the last stick on the fire. The Great Spirit provided wood free for taking. Individuals and communities worked out a simplicity of living, which reduced complexities to workable solutions for all. Then almost overnight, these semi-nomads, thrown into contact with bewildered persons of other races, felt like decapitated hens. Their simplicity and trust in nature led them to have the same trust in people of other races. Unfortunately, their first whirling contact with other races (many of whom called themselves Christians) was mercilessly riddled by the result of bootleggers, promiscuous living persons, and other evils. These vices added to their own weaknesses lowered their morale. Their young women were tempted, offered little resistance, and venereal diseases and tuberculosis wrought havoc among them. Such things caused them to lose faith in a race, whose people broke sworn treaties.

Traders and visitors, not satisfied with their greed for material wealth and exploitation, insulted and raped the docile wives and girls. Either from desire or from hospitality obligations, the women offered little resistance for the subtle seducers. Then the men disappeared unpunished by their government, unhampered by conscience, leaving behind germs and illegitimate children for the Indians to raise, which they did with loving care. As a result, we had many of these half-breed children in our School, to pose yet another problem for the authorities.

Throw a stone into a pool of water and the face of the universe will never be quite the same. The place from where the stone was taken is empty. The place where it lands is not its original home. One life may be no more than a ripple in the great cosmos, but one ripple causes another, then another, which may cause great chaos. Vibration changes the position (one eighth of an inch off-balance) of a snowberg, a city is wiped out, and the surface of the earth is greatly changed. We have experienced how historical events can strike just as quickly, but the lasting elements come slowly. Three hundred and twenty-five years intervened between the birth of Christianity and its acceptance as an official religion by some people in the ancient world. I could not help but liken this to the awakening of these Indians. There may be more permanence in the slow awakening than in the speed of some other races, especially in this age of jet propulsion and space travel. The stone, or new seed, has been sown deeply into thinking Indians, and is taking root and growing, as with the Negroes.

Like birds, Indians had as much government as they thought they needed. They remained in one place long enough to get food. Rather than stay in unclean and unpleasant surroundings, they migrated. Spring house-cleaning problems were quickly and easily solved without days of upheaval and frayed nerves by moving their tents from place to place.

It is quite evident that until recently most people looked upon Indians as a dying race, who would not long be a burden to the white government. The situation has changed drastically, and the government is faced with Indian population explosion. Indians, once thought to be doomed, are bouncing back.

The financial burden, no doubt, was uppermost in officials' minds when they decided to feed, clothe, and start to educate Indians. They hoped to change their simple minds. Chiefs had (still have) different opinions and different methods stored in their minds. This anti-intellectual, anti-cultural, and anti-progressive method did not satisfy their needs. They could not accept the white man's way of living, overnight.

When intensely interested in some project the children, and adults, were annoyed and felt it bondage to be stopped on the exact dot of time denoted by one small clock hand. Tokawaka Indians seemed to be able to feast most of the night and sleep all the next day, or vice versa, without it affecting their natures. They could go twenty-four hours without food, gorge, and not have indigestion.

I asked Bill Thomas and John Frank who had just returned from the army how they enjoyed life outside the reservation, and how they liked the men with whom they worked. Bill replied that he had a wonderful time, and met a lot of nice people. He said, 'I liked two young soldiers, Jim Mason and Tom Patterson. Both said that they were studying at the university. I asked them what they were studying. They replied, "We are taking Arts." I did not know what "Arts" meant, so I asked what they intended to do when they finished studying. Jim replied, "I don't know, my father wants me to go into his shoe business with him, but there is no money in that business for me." Tom said, "My father has so much money he does not know how to spend it. I guess I'll go into his office. There is not much work involved, and I will have all the money I want to spend." '

John Frank said, 'Many of the soldiers I met said they had enlisted because they were bored with life and wanted adventure.'

These boys had returned home from the forces with true, or imaginary, tales of meeting students who were bored with life. The chiefs had listened to them, formed their own opinions, and Chief Atlon said, 'We know there are different types of men, but we feel sorry for such young men. They do not know the joy our young men feel in everyday living. The sea challenges them. It means food. There is also satisfaction when we land a big fish or shoot a good seal.'

Tokawaka children, who learned to speak English before they were eight years old, did not have the same trouble that older children had when they were learning English.

School children habitually accepted the regulated School life as part of their compulsory living. Many of them, when they left the School, returned to their homes and relinquished the white man's niceties and routine as quickly and unprotestingly as they accepted the routine. Nonetheless, something happened to their minds during their School years. Many of them will never be satisfied with their fathers' and grandparents' ways of living. On the other hand, the regimented life did not fit them for the drastic change back to the old way of living. For the time being, they are accepting the least line of resistance, and hope that some change will take place. Miracles have happened.

Already on Tokawaka reservation lives are not unnecessarily lost by tribal or racial warfare. They no longer have indefinite periods of desperate starvation. Epidemics, except for venereal diseases and tuberculosis, do not run rampant as they did in the nomadic days.

But they face complex problems in their family and community life. They want unity retained. With their children taken from them, they see their homes and communities being ruthlessly upset, the feeling of friendliness and hospitality of their village life is more valuable to them than too much efficiency. This makes it difficult for them to believe what they see is for their betterment. It makes it more difficult for them to understand what workers among them are teaching, especially when some of them teach one thing, but live by quite a different philosophy of life, not conducive to a practicable way for Indians. Many of the modern ways of living with which they come in contact, may not prove beneficial to their permanent stability (or to any nation), in which home influence should be the foundation. Until they can see a better way offered to them, the chiefs think that they can best retain their stability in their own homes, under parental influence. They may not be too far wrong. Their home seems to be vitally needed, as an anchor, a safe haven, where they can find fun, fellowship, and love; where they can put aside cares and burdens, and find understanding and companionship with their children.

Seventy-year-old Chief Mungo Martin, the famous totem pole carver, is reported to have said, 'White man's ways no good. White man is always preaching this, but never doing it.' Through Chief Atlon, Chief Swan made a similar statement. He said:

'We believe in sharing goods with one another. We do not believe in the accumulation of private goods and wealth. The white man is always preaching this, but never doing it. We live day by day, and we believe that tomorrow will take care of itself. The white man is always worrying about the future, which may never come. He never enjoys each day.'

CHAPTER 11

TOTEM

Three imposing, brilliantly painted totem poles attracted my eye. The first thing to catch a visitor's eye when approaching the village.

I had read that each tribe was the proud owner of a crest – the same idea as the European coat of arms, but curiosity prompted me to ask Gladys why Tokawaka had three poles. She explained that in olden days tribes fought among themselves. Sometimes only a few men of one tribe remained alive. The captured prisoners had to accept as their leader the chief of the victorious tribe. The height of a pole denoted the highest rank. The number of figures, the greater knowledge and longer ancestry. Chief Swan's pole was the tallest one, with the bright figures carved and painted on it. He had his legs broken and was badly crippled so he had to crawl about the floor and had to be carried to the boats. As a tribe needs a strong man as chief, he made his son, Chief Atlon, acting chief, although Chief Swan's word was law and he was consulted on all events.

Chief Kenderson's father was a chief taken prisoner by this tribe. As they always show consideration for a chief who is taken prisoner, his son became chief when his father died. He had married a princess in the tribe (now dead). His totem pole was shorter with fewer figures carved on it. Chief Atlon's pole was similar to his father's pole, between the other two. These totem poles had elaborately carved grotesque figures painted in gaudy colours.

It was marvellous draughtsmanship as most British Columbian poles are.

I was intrigued by the unique, picturesque figures, which represented real or imaginary birds, beings, and beasts, which had long beaks and outstanding wings.

In answer to my questions, Gladys explained that the carvings were what they called marks of distinction to commemorate bravery and ancestry. They also signified social standing and achievements of chiefs and their families. A 'totem' in all parts of the world is something representing ancestral heritage, which the people are taught to reverence, and Chief Atlon explained that to them the poles were heraldic emblems, like family crests. That they depicted the achievements and the lineage of the owners – partly legendary. The long wings, curved, straight beaks, and other peculiar quirks represented persons with symbolic touches. Such figures were conventionalised and exaggerated, but they were identified with human beings and animals. Once a pole was carved and erected no one was allowed to alter it without having a potlatch to explain the reason for the change. No doubt, that accounts for many old poles found in parts of British Columbia. It was cheaper to erect new poles than to hold a potlatch and get permission to change an old pole. Other uses for totem poles in some tribes were as memorials to the dead or to celebrate victory over an opponent.

I asked if the thunderbird, which plays such a large part in Indian traditions, in this tribe particularly, ever existed. Chief Atlon said that his grandfather told him that the Thunderbird got its name from thunder, which was thought to be made from the flap of its wings. Lightning flashed from its eyes. Its beak had the power to harpoon whales and carry them away to the mountain top to devour.

Straight-grained, native red cedar is soft, chips easily and lends itself to carving purposes. Men and boys, skilled craftsmen, carved beautiful figures and totem poles. Peter was a clever wood carver. These Indians held the eagle, the most important figure, in awe. The thunderbird was considered a lifesaver, or protector. The killer whale represented the defeated enemy. Although the thunderbird was legendary, many stories were told about it, the whale and the fish. They were interwoven with the wolf, which symbolized cunning. The grizzly bear symbolized strength.

Early missionaries considered these poles idolatrous and tried to destroy them. Scientists today believe these carvings may enlighten us on past Indian history.

John remarked, 'I wonder if some of their weird carvings

represent the scalping of your and my great-great-grand-parents? Have Indians kept these trophies or remembrances of long past power victories to show wealth and power, as we pre-serve trophies of our victories over other nations, so that our children may see them in museums?'

I saw a photograph recently showing a totem pole one hundred and twenty-five feet high, cut from a one hundred and fifty feet tall cedar, over two hundred years old. It took Chief Mungo Martin, one of the oldest and most famed carvers of the British Columbia coast, his son and nephew, three months to carve the pole from legends from his ancestors. According to Chief Martin, there was a popular legend that not long after the Great Flood, Greeksem, the founder of his clan, living alone on the shore of Vancouver Island, heard strange cries and was surprised to see a pole, later called a totem pole, rising up from the beach. He was more surprised to see a man, Baguanum, speaking from the bottom of the pole. He told him that he was to wear a ring of cedar around his neck and that the pole figures would be clan crests. The animal crests have been used ever since. Thus the low man on Mr Martin's pole represents Greeksem, but this is the first time all of them have been carved on one pole. The tremendous work of art, representing the Kwakiutl tribal colours, stands in Victoria Beach Hill Park. It is predicted that this pole will last at least five hundred years, and Indian history will not be lost.

The totem pole, the religious and tribal emblem of North American Indians, was on the new Canadian silver dollar to commemorate the 100th anniversary of the creation of British Columbia.

Perhaps Indians are beginning to receive credit for what they have contributed to North America.

Women on the Tokawaka reservation excel in making baskets with intricately designed, finely woven reeds. As I watched Nellie and Gladys dyeing reeds, I asked them from what source they derived their colours. Nellie explained that she made some of the brilliant colours from roots and herbs; the light and soft shades, from early birch bark. The delicate yellow shade was from ash bark; the dark brown from pine bark. The previous fall she had boiled blueberries to make the purplish red. Rotting wood was used for the darker shades of blue; cedar bark for the bright shades of green. She made pearly-blue-grey shades, from shredded bark, roots, and berries of sumac. And I learned that nearly any shade could be made by mixing earth with other colours.

When I asked if home dyed colours faded more quickly than store dyes, she assured me that they do not fade as quickly and that they do not have money to buy dyes.

These women took pride in their work, were pleased to have someone admire it, and eager to answer questions. Intrigued at their ingenuity, especially in making so many colours from almost nothing, I played truant, with a clear conscience. Nellie brought out her woven, cedar bark mats, used for many purposes; curtains, floor rugs, table clothes, bed, and boats. In answer to my questions as to where she got the designs, Gladys tugged out a wooden box from under her bed. She delved into its depth and brought forth a large piece of gunny sack, with dozens of designs stamped on it and said, 'The eldest girl in each better class family receives this ancestral, gunny sack of designs, brought from generation to generation. I am the eldest girl in my family.'

I recalled Peter's explanation about his grandmother's teeth designs. No wonder Indian women had good teeth.

Gladys continued, 'The mystical legends of the figures date back so far none of my people know their origin. But like Biblical stories they come from some main source. They are more or less legends about our people. They are also more than history because they are based on things of a world beyond our seeing eyes, to let us know that the world is real, and that nothing is impossible with our Great Spirit.'

It was evident that the source of these imaginative, fascinating designs, woven into the gunny sack, which had been passed down for many generations, will always be a mystery. These mystical legends link the vivid past with the immortal past, until they are so interwoven with their religion, it is difficult for outsiders (and perhaps younger Indians) to define the line of demarcation.

Later when Sarah, an orphan in the School, showed me her gunny sack of designs, which she treasured more than anything

115

else she owned, even more than her new clothes, I realized the value of her heirloom.

When Gladys showed me some fine and beautiful bead work; armbands, centre pieces, belts, and vases, with the same patterns, I was curious to know why the thunderbird, canoe, and Indians were frantically pushing the oars, with the whale near by, in all their designs. She explained that the design was what we call sacred. Her grandfather had told her that Indians in most parts of Canada had it on all their work. He said that once at some bay, at an encampment, people were in a starving condition. Quannis, the killer whale, swam back and forth in front of the bay and kept the fish from coming in. All of the men, except a small boy, and Skeecullus, the Thinker with the withered hand, went with the warriors to kill Quannis. They returned empty handed. Then, Skeecullus spoke and said that it was not the fault of the warriors or the spears. It was Quannis casting evil spells over the fish so that they were able to throw aside the spears. The chiefs laughed and sent for their Saauch friends to join them. Skeecullus saw it was useless to argue.

The Saauch friends joined them, but a great sickness and weariness came over them, and they were unable to launch their canoes. No one knew what to do but Skeecullus. He said, ' Tis Quannis' wicked spells that make the hunters sick. Stop boasting and ask Tzinquay, the Thunderbird, what to do. Send for Schnayn, the medicine man.'

They did. He came and made them strong with medicine. Then, his magic cry and the cries of the people, which reached Tzinquay, where he lived beyond the mountains, brought help to them.

While the people bowed their heads, asking for help, the shadow of the thunderbird winged its way down the narrows. There was a terrific clap of thunder, and Tzinquay swooped down on Quannis, swimming to and fro across the mouth of the bay. The killer whale threshed about in the water. The noise of battle was terrific. The great thunderbird flew over- head, carrying the dead Quannis in his talons. He flew lower and lower, and dropped the dead body at their feet. The salmon came in. They had a great feast, but they never forgot what Tzanquay had done for them. They made pictures and scenes on their canoes, wove them into basket designs, knit them into sweaters, worked them into bead articles, and carved them on poles. 'The design is to remind all Indians for all times, that we should never be boastful, but that we should remain humble.'

She had told the story so many times, she knew it word for word.

Tokawaka Indian religion, developed from nature, is closely associated with the deep, underlying elements, connected with their mystical legends. They believe that everything in nature, the sea, the wind, the sun, the trees, the bear, the fox, and all birds have souls, and that supernatural beings surround them on all sides, in the woods, air, and water. Unlike many of us, they openly profess to a Higher Ruler, speak openly of their dependence on their Great Spirit, and accept Him as ruler of the universe and their lives.

There is a stupendous distance between St Paul's Cathedral, our large North American churches, and the teepees and homes of Tokawaka Indians. There is also a vast difference between the reverent worshippers who kneel beside the throbbing of the mighty waters in the depth of the silent fir forest, and under the candescent world of awe-inspiring stars, and those who kneel in padded pews, in richly adorned cathedrals and churches, but there is only One who knows which worshippers are the most sincere in their hearts.

After dinner one day, the children had been marshalled into the class rooms, and I stole upstairs for sixty winks.

I had scarcely closed my eyes before Norah shouted up, 'Classes are dismissed for the afternoon. We are all invited to Bertha's Christian wedding.'

The previous year, Bertha, a recent School girl, had consummated an Indian marriage by cohabiting with a man. By the time her daughter was three months old, Bertha had taken time to think things over. A pricked conscience, Mr King's persuasion, or the thought that she might be more eligible to participate in mission bale handouts, made her decide to go through a Christian wedding service.

Mr King droned through the proper ritual. The bride and groom made the required responsive promises. 'Bring up your children in the Christian way; live with each other only.' The service ended, and Chief Atlon announced, 'Chief Swan invites all of you to his home.'

The walls of the chief's large room were lined with School children sitting on benches or squatting on the floor. The room fairly bulged with people. Bertha, sitting beside her mother, held Lena on her lap. Chief Swan sitting on his dais, surrounded by her wedding presents, announced, 'We celebrate Bertha's Christian wedding.'

He held high a red and white piece of gingham, and announced, 'Martha's gift to Bertha.'

Bertha shifted Lena to her grandmother's lap, walked up, took the gingham, bowed, looked at Martha, nodded, 'Thank you,' and walked back to her bench.

Chief Swan held up a brown teapot, and called out, 'Jennie's gift to Bertha.' His announcements and her reception of gifts continued until all had been received; apron, towel, cup and saucer, baby's rattle, doll, pillow case, and other articles. The moment Bertha accepted the last gift, women and girls gathered about her, felt, admired, and asked the price of each article; not merely curious, just friendly interest.

A recent announcement stated that Indians are not compelled to register their marriages with the provincial government, it will recognize Indian marriages registered with the federal government. Chiefs have won one point. This statement made me wonder it would have been better to have left these young people to enjoy the contentment and satisfaction of their primitive ancestors? Would this Christian wedding help to push them too quickly into the age of irritation? An age in which spiritual and physical satisfactions seem to be sought, but not found by so many of the assembly-line workers.

The chiefs know that their young people must learn, for their own good, to mix with people of other races, and that they must stand on their own feet. Yet I could not see Big John or Peter, with the upbringing of their ancestors indelibly on their minds, as assembly-line workers. I could not picture them contented to screw a similar nut on a similar bolt, day after day, living their repressed lives, with its withering effect on all their natural satisfaction; in an office, Peter's soul would be poverty stricken.

I often thought of the Tokawaka Indians when I heard the psalm :

> 'They that go down to the sea in ships, that do business in great waters. These see the works of the Lord and His wonders in the deep.'

As we discussed Bertha's wedding, we recalled how irritation and discouragements eventually make men vent their pent-up feelings upon neighbours, wives, and children, when that fails, upon the very industry which has made them inhuman slaves, scarcely above the level of animals, chained to the treadmill. We were concerned about some of the things we were introducing to these School children, which may provide dangerous pitfalls when they are forced into such environments as mentioned here.

After Bertha's wedding, I found it a little more difficult to picture Indians integrated and assimilated, finding satisfaction in such a mechanical civilization into which they must soon take their places. I thought of people I knew lost in the mechanical mob, doing jobs over and over, until they lost the satisfaction and happiness enjoyed by the old-time farmer and small businessman, with their independence, dignity, initiative, and pride in achievement. It made me sad to think what might happen to the spirits of these happy, innocent, lovable papooses. Yet, it is impossible to stop progress. Drastic changes will soon effect the lives of these children, no doubt, for their own good. But surrounded by overwhelming aggressive white races would they retain their identity, which they have retained for over four thousand years?

Chiefs have striven to keep their people from entering into the main stream of European life which flows around them, selecting only what they want in their everyday environment. Although generation after generation of youth have had to face similar die-hard conditions, and have had to adjust themselves into the quagmire of justice, injustice, and evil, they have not had to adjust themselves in the way Bertha's children and grandchildren, and hundreds of other young School children will have to do if they continue to live happily married lives.

Civilization expands. It is necessary to erect huge buildings –

119

many times haphazardly as a result of the mechanical – industrial cycle. The larger the building or the city the more frustration and annoyances are encountered, until many men, who build these buildings, are forced to pay high rent or live in cramped and sordid homes. Will integration force this situation on young Indians? Will they lose the quiet serenity of communal life? If they are to retain their happy personalities, when integrated in huge masses of people, serenity is a must.

One Indian remarked that the time had come for his people to unite in a common effort to destroy the untruths and persecutions which had followed them from the moment they were born, because injustice has a way of worming itself into souls, until temptation becomes too much for that soul.

It was strange that there was really no juvenile delinquency on the reservation, drunkenness at times, but no real alcoholics. There were no 'jungles' where outcasts gathered; no outcasts. There were no narcotic addictions, no psychopaths, outrageous sex murders, few nervous disorders, and a low rate of mental patients. There was respect for the aged and the infirm.

The old Indian law, stating that all women and children go in safety, is still adhered to.

Unfortunately, no definite programme has been presented to the federal government regarding the behaviour and morals of white people visiting this reservation.

CHAPTER 12

THE BOOTLEGGER CALLS

Two or three families lived in many of the houses. Few Indians were blessed with many household goods. When the canneries opened, they bundled everything they needed – feather mattresses, cedar rugs, boots, pans, flour, dogs, and babies – into their boats and moved to the canneries. The better class Indians carried their belongings about in huge, cleverly constructed chests, with delicate and intricate carvings.

I never heard, 'Don't scratch the chairs!' 'Stop marking the wall paper!' or 'Keep your dirty shoes off the cushions!' Drab homes, without paint or wall paper, chairs or chesterfields, exempted their children from innumerable petty restrictions.

Pre-school age children went barefoot. Adults sat on benches. Papooses, free from constant nagging and scolding, which tend to make nervous children, with a tendency to develop into neurotic adults, enjoyed more freedom than do most white children. Without some of these niceties they did not learn to appreciate a beautiful home.

The children usually ruled the home. Not in the same manner that a spoiled child runs over many a modern parent, who camouflages her indifference, or laziness, by calling it a 'new philosophy' – Junior expressing himself – regardless of other peoples' feelings or destruction of property.

I never saw an Indian mother strike her child. These children seemed to learn early in life that tears were a sign of weakness. They rarely shed tears. Some of them did cry until they got what they wanted. Yet they were never a nuisance. At a fantastically young age the children in a canoe did as they were told, quickly, and without fuss. There was no corporal punishment, hasty blows or unkind words, with their distasteful lasting effects.

121

The smallness of this reservation (and many others), a closely knit band, made individual lives an open book to neighbours. Every adult was interested in each child. When a child suffered disgrace or feeling of pride no private chastisement in the home had the same effect as the outspoken reproof of the chief, or the entire community. This community interest of the individual, with its profound and lasting effect on every man, woman, and child, at every period of life, will be lost in city life. On the other hand, it did not fit the children for the bewildering home and social environments any who leave reservation life are bound to encounter.

Until many of the children were two or three years old, clothing, especially during warm weather, was worn for protection only, not from modesty. They were not hampered by many, if any, clothes. Nude papooses bathed and swam in the salt water summer and winter.

Gladys told me that before a girl is of School age her ears are pierced. This ceremony entails traditional significance, fraught with mystery and danger, during which some supernatural power draws near and marks her destiny. She would not give me any details of the significance of the ceremony.

Tokawaka Indians had little political consciousness. The celebate state was scorned; marriage was secondary and entailed little romance. Men married when they were about eighteen or nineteen; girls, when seventeen or eighteen, or even younger.

When the teachers and I first worked with Indians, we became impatient at the slow-thinking replies to our questions. Later, I recalled a prominent psychiatrist, Dr Ross, saying, as he stood by the bedside of a restless business woman, 'I never heard of a Jersey cow running a temperature because her boy friend was running around with another heifer. She stood calmly meditating and chewing her cud. Even the cow seems to know that tomorrow will take care of itself.' I wondered if he was thinking of the Indians.

Eventually, we could sit and wait, without being impatient, for an Indian to think and act.

I might have given up the whole effort but for another remark which I recalled having heard Dr Ross make. It upheld me throughout these trying months. 'Seek worthwhile things because even if you own the whole world, you can sleep in only one bed at night and eat only so much each day.'

When the children were safely locked in their dormitories, the teachers and I discussed the doings of the day and the conditions under which we were compelled to work. When contrasting Indians' problems with world problems, John quoted Thoreau's statement; 'Man who is happiest is the one whose pleasures are cheapest.'

Gladys had brought about this discussion. She said that when white men travelled they had to tote a lot things along with them. Compared with Indians, this is quite true. White men seem lost, either naturally or by assumed superiority, without an abundance of canned foods, clothes, a car, etc., and all modern conveniences, including an electric razor.

John remarked, 'I envy the Indian. He never has to shave.'

We could not picture Big John, spiritually water-logged, knocking a tiny golf ball around a field, then hiring a caddy to run after it. He would grunt, 'Senseless.' Many of these Indians gave me the impression that they felt it useless to perform unnecessary manual labour. Instead of hitting a golf ball, he would sit and meditate, or take himself off to another reservation, in the clothes he was wearing, unhindered by baggage. There, he would swap yarns for hours or days. Or, if he really needed exercise he would go out and shoot a seal or catch a fish for a good meal.

We agreed with John that we had never seen a youth like Peter. He never tired of sitting on a rock gazing on the sky, the stars, the sun, the trees, and the birds, 'meditating on the Great Spirit back of them.'

Often he nonplussed John with his questions. 'Do you know Tom said that when he was in the army he heard the government, or someone, spends thousands of dollars for buses to carry children, who should be walking to school. Then it spends thousands of dollars to build places for the same children to take exercise to keep them healthy and to develop their muscles. Sounds crazy to me! Is it true?'

According to our standards, these six year old children, taken from their parents and regimented into the School until they are fifteen, were in a much better environment than if they

123

had been left on the reservation. But during this important formation period of their lives, the suppression of their natural, emotional makeup made many of them rebel against the repression of their spontaneous, intellectual thinking and response. Personalities were dwarfed and individual indentity lost in the regimentation, and regained when the children returned to their home life.

Readers who have read Monica Baldwin's book, *I Leap over the Wall,* will have a better understanding of the feeling of these Tokawaka Indians. This young convert novice took the vow and became a nun. For twenty years her seniors watched her like a cat watches a mouse. During all those years, she lived virtually in the fourteenth century, in discipline and environment. She lived on almost less than the bare necessities of life, wore plain, homespun clothing, and was allowed to speak only at certain intervals. The day came when she could not stand the mental and physical strain. She stepped from such an environment into the modern, speed-nerve-wrecked world of 1941. She was stunned and almost overwhelmed at the change.

Descendants of Indians, taken from free roaming lands and placed in restricted environment, have to contend with just such overwhelming conditions.

I was forced to admit another stickler for them. They think it meaningless to sweat and labour to provide a luxurious layette for a baby. Especially if it meant that the father would never have time to enjoy his baby, who wore the fine clothes.

Most mothers provided the bare necessities; wash basin, cake of laundry soap, a rag for a wash cloth, a dress or two, three or four diapers, and a blanket. Birth, a natural function, did not cause undue commotion. From early infancy children were the companions of their parents, and toddled behind them, learning by experience and observation. As I watched them, I often wondered if they were growing up in a more civilized world than many children of white parents, who have to send their children to the movie, *Mum and Dad,* to learn the facts of life.

Chief Kenderson, inclined to be jealous of some of the white man's possessions and privileges, shrugged his shoulders, and remarked, 'White men gorge daily, but they never know the blissful sensation that comes to our stomachs after a long seal blubber feast: especially after days of dried clams, bannock, and tea. It is only when we are hungry for days for a taste of seal that we can shout joyously, "I got a seal." '

We may not get as much satisfaction as Indians from eating, but seal blubber and its grease definitely did not tempt me. I recalled what Peter's grandfather, with his inborn longing for buffalo steak, had said, and I realized that our tastes differed.

I mulled over Chief Atlon's statement. 'No government officials, who have never endured stern tests, cold, hunger, and outdoor hardships, can direct Indian affairs and give, and get, the most beneficial results. We have been hungry, cold, and in danger. We have had to use every bit of strength in our bodies and every brain in our heads wrestling with nature on land and on the water.'

The teachers and I, many times, were inclined to agree with this wise chief. A government man, who sits in an office, cannot possibly understand this life, without consulting chiefs, any more than the chief could know how to tell him to run his office.

I threaded my way along the narrow village path, followed by two mangy dogs, too thin to bark. Suddenly, I heard loud threats and was confronted by tousle-headed Liz, her naked shoulders protruding through the tatters of her dirty blouse. With snapping eyes and shaking her fists, she was gesticulating to someone inside the window. The moment she saw me she snapped shut quicker than a clam, and shuffled behind the old shed. A group of men and women, peeking around the door in the next house, disappeared as if by magic.

I had, to my sorrow, discovered that a nurse's duties on this reservation was multifarious. Forced, against my will, I had to accept the responsibility of reporting intoxicated Indians. I wanted to learn the true facts before I went into Liz and Don's home. Every Indian knew that it was a punishable offence to withhold legitimate information from the nurse. I questioned two women in the next home. They shrugged their shoulders and looked blank. Eventually, through a series of unintelligent answers, I got a fairly coherent account of what had happened.

'Dan got moonshine. 'Twas not his fault.'

'The white bootlegger sold it to him.'

'He threw Liz out the window. She's to blame. She's always nagging him.'

'If Liz had left him alone, he would have been all right.'

' 'Twas the bootleggers' fault for bringing liquor.'

I heard Frank Thomas mutter, 'Punish the white bootlegger.'

My sympathy was with Dan. I had been tempted many times to take Liz, Dan's second wife, by the nape of the neck and shake some sense into her. But it was my duty to report Dan's intoxicated state to the proper authorities. He would have to be punished, while the white bootlegger would sneak away unpunished to another harbour and continue his illegal, destructive work. And there no doubt more Indians would be punished. They had to accept this procedure the white man's law, called justice.

Dan accused of being intoxicated and abusing his wife was sentenced to three weeks in jail. Knowing she would have to dig for herself without receiving any sympathy, Liz changed her tactics. She sought the police, and explained that they were having a friendly husband-wife spat.

The police contended that there was too much spat and too little friendliness.

Liz wept crocodile tears and carried on the rest of the day. There was no jail on this reservation so Dan was taken away. In a few days the event was forgotten for the time being.

Two and a half weeks later, at three o'clock, one morning, I was awakened by someone pounding on the children's dining-room door. I crawled out of my warm bed, shoved my feet into my sealskin slippers, went downstairs, and pushed back the slide of the peep-hole in the locked door, and looked through. An Indian shone his flashlight rays through the hole, and announced, 'I have come for you. Frank's Tommy is dying.' Although his voice was familiar, the light was too dim to recognize his face.

Papooses are such peculiar youngsters, bright, apparently strong one moment, gone the next, it was difficult to make a definite diagnosis or prognosis. I had informed Mr King that I feared he would not be with us much longer. Inherited venereal disease and tuberculosis had eaten away his skeleton body. His

126

parents knew we could not save him but, like all parents, they hoped I might do something, and they wanted me.

The night was Stygian black. A weird wind moaned through the furze. Rain spat in our faces. Thunder growled and zig-zags of lightning cut through the sky. We skidded silently along the boardwalk. When we were about half way through the bush, he stopped, and asked, 'Do you remember me?' I recognized his voice instantly, and my heart leaped into my mouth. My hair sprouted upwards and a chill ran down my spine. This was an ideal spot for revenge.

A cougar's hungry cry pierced the air. My skin prickled, and a clammy sweat broke over my forehead. What an ending! A lonely spot; the dead of the night! A cougar waiting eager to clear away tell-tale evidence. The subtle mind of an Indian to plan such a night and such an ideal spot.

In a split second, I felt limp as lukewarm water. Then he continued, 'I am Dan. You sent me down to jail. I'll never do it again. They hung two Indians while I was there, and they let me out three days before my time was up. They said it was on account of my good behaviour, but I know it was to save paying my passage money. I came home free on an Indian boat.'

I breathed easier. I was dealing with an Indian, who knew that I was merely doing my duty. He had no revengeful feeling towards me.

When Tommy's suffering ended, Dan with eight other relatives watched me bathe and dress his emaciated body and place it in the tiny homemade box.

Dan and I went silently out into the wet night and skidded along the boardwalk. When we drew near the weird spot, his uncanny sense seemed to surmise my thoughts. He took hold of my arm, and said, 'Just to keep you from slipping off the boards.'

We continued homeward arm in arm, with Dan swinging his flashlight from side to side, to light my footsteps. I felt humble and ashamed at my recent fear of him. During the re-mainder of my stay in Tokawaka, Dan was my staunch friend. I wish I could end by saying that he never again touched moon-shine. Never again did I have to report him.

127

CHAPTER 13

JUST ONE OF THOSE DAYS

Another unforgettable day stands out vividly in my mind.

Barked knees, stubbed toes, drops in stuffy noses, iodine daubed on nasty scratches, old Band-Aids removed, and new ones put on and the last child was shooed off to the class room. At nine o'clock, I locked the dispensary door, left Freddie shovelling sand into his bottle, and set out for the village.

A crystal white hoar frost made the boardwalk treacherous. An invigorating, soft breeze rustled and purred through the furze. Half way through the wood, a friendly squirrel darted from the underbrush in front of me. Chattering to himself, his bushy tail twitching over his back, he scampered to a safe distance up a near fir tree. He stopped, head downwards, clinging to the bark, and scolded me for distracting him in his delicious state of activity, and for intruding into his silent domain.

This sociable yet pugnacious bundle of dynamic energy precipitated head downwards. I chattered back to him. Then as I inched my way along the treacherous, frosty walk, I drank in the natural beauty, little suspecting what awaited me at the end of the trail.

The delightful warmth, so scarce at this time of the year in this part of the province, shone through the open spaces beyond the trees, absorbing some of the chill from the air. Just beyond the wood, the tide inched higher and higher up the rocks. Salt waves gently lapped the sandy beach. Far above the trees, a brilliant blue sky looked down. High up in the clouds, a majestic, white-headed eagle soared across the horizon. The exhilarating twang in the salt breeze brought nostalgic memories of the seashore, which, as now, always intoxicated me, and lifted my soul and spirit above earth-born cares.

I started along the muddy path and noticed that a previously empty shack was occupied. A woman, with wrinkled face, which appeared to have weathered a hundred years (age unknown), motioned for me to come inside. She could not speak or understand much English, but she took my hand and pulled me across the room to the corner, where a man scarcely recognizable as human was curled up on a stench-reeking cedar mat on the floor. Although he could not speak English, two glazed eyes set in sunken, bronzed sockets, stared at me, appealing for ease to his pain. All the flesh on his body seemed glued to his bones. Dried, yellow skin was stretched tightly over his bony skull. I stooped, inhaled the stench of rotting flesh and fetid air, gagged and barely refrained from retching. My gorge rose and my brain jellied into a quivering reflection of stomach. Those pleading eyes, so like those of a wounded fawn, affected me. To find the source of the odour, I lifted his filthy quilt. The barefoot woman padded round and rolled down the back of his fleece-lined drawers. I had seen many repugnant sores during my nursing career but nothing that compared with the decaying hole at the base of his spine. Infected bone protruded through the rotting flesh. An area large as a saucer lined with decaying flesh, exuding pus, gave off a rotten, putrid odour. It was surrounded by caked, weeks-old human excreta. It required all my strength and will power to refrain from registering my personal feelings. By signs and motions, the woman, later known as Skookum Toptent, gave me to understand that she did not have any clean clothes or bedding to replace the filthy quilt and under-clothing. Before treating such a sore I would have to kneel on the flea-infested, plank floor and use basins of lysol-water and green soap lather. Would the patient stand the strain? Would he live days or weeks? Would he live through a bath? Indians are peculiar (perhaps no different to people of other races) when their own peoples' interests are infringed on by outsiders. Would they blame me if a bath proved too much of a shock for this old system? I decided to risk a bath.

Providence, as always, helped me out and assumed some of the responsibility. While puzzling my brain, Jessie came running along the path, shouting, 'Lawrence is in one of his fits.'

First things had to come first. Lawrence's fit, nothing unusual, was not a cause for excitement. This uneducated, twelve year old epileptic, victim of venereal and tubercular infection ravages, had seizures which prohibited him entering the School. I had asked his mother to let me know when he had the next seizure.

Pushing aside the bathing episode for later consideration, I followed Jessie to Lawrence's home. It was not Friday the thirteenth, and no black cat had crossed my path. It was just one of those days when everything happened. Lawrence was barely out of his fit when Gladys strolled in, and remarked, 'Melinda had a baby awhile ago. She is alone, perhaps you should go and see that she is all right.'

Melinda's three year old Clarissa sat on the floor, holding a nude, newborn baby. One end of the blanket was partially wrapped around the body, the other, trailed on the floor. Melinda's husband was away fishing, and the rest of her children were in the School. There was no excitement. She had given birth to her baby, chewed off the cord, given the baby to Clarissa, and crawled into the bunk for a short rest.

During my nurse-training days, doctors had warned us that if the cord was not properly tied any baby could bleed to death in a few moments, and that it was the nurses' duty to watch newborn babies very closely for such bleeding. This pink baby born over an hour before had no intention of bleeding to death. I tied off the cord, slipped on the baby's only one-piece dress and tucked her in beside her mother. Josie and Tillie, who had watched many babies being born, wandered in – from curiosity and neighbourliness.

I left the mother and baby in their care, and crossed the ditch to the next home. *En route,* I met eleven year old Johnny, leading his blind grandmother, Skookum Annie. Johnny, a pathetic boy, left an orphan when his mother died, could not enter the School. Pus from incurable tubercular glands always seemed to be running down his neck and shoulders. The doctor considered sun and air better for the sore than filthy clothes – no dressings available. While his father was away fishing, Johnny and Skookum Annie cared for each other. Whenever I met the pair, Johnny said, 'Look, see today better.'

To please him, I always examined his sores, gave Skookum Annie a few encouraging pats, which she understood, and they continued their roaming.

I believe that patients should face situations squarely. But knowing how many times diagnosis can prove wrong and discouraging – especially with long months ahead – I felt justified in encouraging these two pathetic patients with a few days, or a few weeks.

Eleven-thirty! Just time to investigate the bathing problem, have dinner, and return with a full stomach to tackle the job.

Gladys informed me that Tillicum Toptent's legs were so badly crippled he could not walk. All summer to help him pass the time, his wife and sons had dragged him about from tent to boat. They could not take him out sealing, and he wanted to be in his own home to die, so they had brought him home. They did not think he could live much longer.

Discouraged, sick at heart over the suffering of humanity, I forced myself along the boardwalk. I just could not recapture the enthusiasm and beauty of the morning. So much had happened in such a short time, it hardly seemed possible that it could be the same forenoon, the same wood, and the same world. Even the friendly squirrel had disappeared. But one friend never failed me. Freddie met me, grinning from ear to ear, his bottle full of sand, and lisped, 'Full.'

Jeannie ran down the walk, shouting, 'Mr Brant, dinner, Mr King say, good, five cents. Freddie be good.'

'I good, get cents,' repeated Freddie.

A weight was lifted from my mind. Tillicum Toptent's clothing problem would be solved, Mr Brant had authority to issue the necessary clothing. Tillicum could be made clean and more comfortable, nevertheless, I was doomed for a disappointment.

He insisted that blankets were only issued on death, and my request was refused. But kind-hearted Mrs King motioned for me to come into the well-filled storeroom, and gave me a blanket and a pair of pyjamas. I started off for the village fortified with the clean clothing, a bottle of lysol, and one of green soap. The same natural beauty surrounded me, but I could not work up enthusiasm. There was no friendly squirrel to greet me. I thought to myself, how much external beauty depends on the mood of the inner self – or vice versa.

Several men and women, squatting about the room, watched me give that bath. With much grunting and tugging Big John,

131

his wife, and I managed to peel off Tillicum's underclothing and pull fresh clothing over as clean a body as green soap, lysol, and elbow grease could give him. Afterwards, I wrapped him in his begrudged blanket. By gestures I made his wife understand that I would not come again unless she scrubbed the floor, cleaned up the house, and washed the filthy clothes and bedding.

The next morning, she greeted me with beaming face, and pointed to a heap of clean clothes on the floor. I began to think, perhaps, Mr Brant knew Indians better than I did. Someone had come across with another set of underwear and a blanket. When I saw his trousers and cedar mat scrubbed clean, piled in the corner, a midnight dip in the sulphur spring lost most of its appeal.

Although his loathsome sore never healed, with disinfectants I managed to keep down the stench sufficiently to make nursing care possible. I sat on the floor beside him while he drew his last breath. Just before he passed on, tears filled his glazed eyes, and I could read an unspoken expression of appreciation in them, which he would carry to his Great Spirit. Tears filled my eyes; but I gave a sigh of relief – not one of the Indians blamed me for killing him with too much bathing.

An hour later, Big John, Chief Atlon, Dan, and Frank Thomas wrapped his blanket, death-fashion, about his body and lifted it into the waiting, homemade, wooden box. They passed it out through the window and carried it over the trail to the beach cemetery. There was no procession of sympathizing neighbours, with well meant remarks, to pass in front of the coffin. Wailing replaced the sympathizing remarks. During the next two days, the wailing of the old women could be heard a quarter of a mile away. This wailing was the Indians' idea of comforting the departed one letting him know that he was missed and lamented.

CHAPTER 14

SPORTS DAY

The life of a papoose in a residential School is a regimented
vacuum compared with that of a child in a loving home. From
the time a child is placed in the School, at six years, or younger,
until he is fourteen or fifteen years old, he lives a supervised,
disciplined, regimented life, twenty-four hours of the day.

A week after Freddie was admitted, I met him stalking along,
proudly grinning from ear to ear, carrying a tiny piece of
crumpled paper for the garbage tin. He announced, 'I has duties
does.' This was one of his first English sentences.

The older boys studied in the class room half days, alternating
weekly, working outside; odd jobs connected with operating
the buildings and grounds. The girls studied similarly, washing,
ironing, mending, sewing, making clothes, dishwashing, sweep-
ing, scrubbing, vegetable preparing, table setting, and cooking
most of the children's food.

The younger children spent part of their school period pick-
ing red cranberries, which grew in abundance on the mossy rocks,
and blackberries, from thorny bushes. These were eaten fresh
and preserved for winter use.

The children welcomed any excuse to be out of the class rooms.
John said, 'These youngsters never really enjoy this artificial
childhood life. Natural instinct for the wild life is uppermost
in the boys' minds.'

These residential School children's lives were regimented by
bells; rising, work, school recess, recreation, supper, prayers,
and all-in dormitory bells. They were under constant supervision from the time the dormitory bell rang at six or six-thirty
in the morning, until they were locked in at nine o'clock. They
worked and played by bells, and knew that even while they
were sleeping they were under the eagle eye of some teacher or
matron. This peep-hole system, similar to that in a psychiatric's

133

cell, was not conducive of a trustful atmosphere for fourteen or fifteen year old children – old enough to be married.

Most people talk about 'My possessions.' Indians may be the only race of people who refer to their possessions and communal belongings as 'Ours'. Previous to the establishment of Schools, no doubt, this was true. In the School where individuality of the child is soon submerged in the herd, it is doubly true.

During the formative years of their lives, these children lacked the individual touch, or a definite place in their mothers' or fathers' affections, enjoyed by most children. Each supervisor had to have easy access to new children. Thus, the new child, on admission, slept in the bed nearest the door in the six-to-nine, nine-to-twelve, twelve-to-fifteen year olds dormitories. Thus a new admission made shifts all along the line. The same advancing scale was used in the dining-room.

Most children in North America have their own clothes. Parents brought a child a dress or sweater occasionally. Each girl received a complete set of new (supposed to be new) clothes on admission. Thereafter each year when she returned from vacation, her old clothes were taken away, and she was outfitted with pass-on or new clothing. Many garments came down from child to child until they dropped to pieces. Most of the girls grew rapidly, and nearly every six months they shed their clothing to the next smaller girl or boy and took the clothes outgrown by the next larger ones.

John told us about discussing with the boys the benefits and handicaps of worldly possessions. As an illustration, he told them the story about the ambitious, energetic spider, that spun a web on a rafter of an old barn. Day after day, suspended from the single rafter thread, which he had spun downward to the sunny window ledge, he spun back and forth, until he had a most beautiful web. Flies, mosquitoes, moths, and insects of all sizes, came to the doorway and never got away. Food for the taking was there. Day after day, he sat dreaming without a care in the world. His stomach stretched to the limit, he grew fatter and lazier. He swung back and forth in his beautiful home. One day, he saw this single thread, and said to himself, 'What is that shining thing hanging from the rafters?' He had forgotten that it was his own work of by-gone days. He thought to himself, 'Something may come down that thread and take some of my food,' so he snipped the thread. His beautiful, fairy web crashed to the floor of the barn, carrying him with it.

The boys listened intently while he told the story. A long silence followed before Peter, with a wise expression on his face, exclaimed, 'How foolish!'

We knew that story would be repeated, meditated on, the moral analysed, and there would be much discussion. During childhood and maturity, these Indians did not judge people by looks or worldly possessions. They did not care a lot whether a person had a cent or a million dollars; whether one was dowdy or stringy as a bean pole. They had learned to appreciate people and respect their friends for their worth and for their reliability. They seemed to respect quality – long may they do so. Their heritage, for hundreds of years, has been spontaneous natural-ness and simplicity, and long may they retain this trait.

The Sunday after John told the story about the spider, I gazed out the church window. My mind wandered back to those natives of North America. What changes would take place on this reservation during the next hundred years?

Indian children, lovers of outdoor sports, threw themselves wholeheartedly into whatever they undertook. Thus, Mr King set aside Sports' Day, similar to an old-fashioned Field Day.

Sports' Day was meaningless to Freddie, except that it meant some exciting eats. Having heard the word so often, each morn-ing, he lisped, 'Today, ports?'

When it arrived, Sports' Day had wings. Before breakfast, the children had finished practically all their work. By ten o'clock, the inside of the School and the campus had received a thorough house cleaning. Jeannie and Freddie, their eyes beam-ing, asked Mrs Grimsby, 'Clean 'nuf, go 'ports?'

The children, one by one, asked leave to go to the beach. Eventually each child, free from routine duties, dressed in Sun-day clothes, went, with a chaperone, to the water's edge. I tagged along with my first-aid kit. As any outsider would be, I was captivated by the wholehearted verve these children were putting into their last minute practice.

Grandparents and parents considered this their children's

day. Stock market and real estate were nonentities. Fishing and housekeeping were forgotten, there would always be another day. This was a day for absolute relaxation. Grandparents, fathers, mothers with babies spread-eagled on their backs, and pre-school age children, squatted on the rocks. Relaxed as poached eggs, many of them had been sitting for hours. Expectancy on their solemn faces would outshine any such expressions on World Exhibitioners.

Gladys informed me that some of them had been there for two hours. When I asked her what she did while waiting, she replied, 'Bill and I were watching two bald headed eagles, wondering what they were doing circling majestically before they disappeared into clouds. We watched the waves breaking on the rocks, and Bill said, "Our Great Spirit has given us an ideal day for this treat." '

The first item on the water sports' programme, a swimming contest, was a marvellous feat. Athletic striplings, clad in trunks only, with arms raised, poised, waited for the word 'start' 'Go', shouted John. Timed to minute precision, each struck the water. Their brown bodies, sleek as seals, cut the waves with rhythmic, even strokes, leaving barely a ripple in their wake. Not a spark of energy was wasted. Each stroke pushed them forward towards their goal, around the out-water marker and back to the beach.

Peter's fingers touched the shore a few seconds before Philip's. Cheers echoed across the water.

These children, like seals, born with the instinct of paddling and rowing, automatically achieved great skill in these arts.

The boys and girls, ready for their favourite water sport, stood alert, their paddles in mid-air, waiting for the signal. The moment John shouted, 'Start', they were off. Their bodies slightly forward and flexed with each stroke. Like all Indians, they paddled with short strokes, which began at the waist and ended with a thrust from the shoulders. Their canoes seemed to fairly skim over the water with almost effortless action.

The second their canoes reached the goal-limit, the boys upset the canoes and paddles into the water; a quick flick of the canoes and they were paddling shoreward.

'Marvellous!' exclaimed Ellen. 'Did you see the way they

capsized and righted their canoes, as though they were boxes on land.'

Slow, dreamy Peter, quickly and quietly leaned across the canoe near the gunnel, tilted it on to its side, rocked it two or three times until all the water spilled over the gunnel. Then, gripping the gunnel firmly, he pulled his body across until he straddled the canoe; wiggled himself side-on into a sitting position, and started paddling shoreward.

I thought to myself that thousands of drowning accidents might be prevented if swimming instructors would insist that canoe-upsetting in water out of their depth, be a part of their pupils' tests.

Tommy's and Bertha's canoe grounded against the sandy beach an inch ahead of Peter's and Stella's canoe. Shouts and cheers re-echoed across the water.

The next stunt, imitating the flight of a weary eagle, was a magnificent sight to behold. Six canoes, a boy and girl in each, shot like an arrow from a bow, swept forward, keeping perfect time. Two quick strokes forward, a rest, alternating with three strokes, a pause, a long rest, followed by a quick splurge shoreward. The moment the canoes scraped the beach, each paddler, representing eagles at the goal, slumped into a complete, sagging, relaxed position.

The last water sports' feat; three boys in each canoe, presented a good imitation of the stealthy manner of approaching night attacks. There was not the slightest sound of a ripple on the water; it was as though one man was paddling.

A signal from Peter brought a blood curdling war whoop. My hair sprouted. Paddles dipped deeply into the water. Foam flew. Each stroke almost lifted the canoes from the water as they made a united dash upon their imaginary enemy.

'Superb! Marvellous!' shouted John.

The winners crowded around Mr King to receive their prizes of candy, chocolate bars and peanuts. Freddie, grinning widely, chocolate from ear to ear, crunching peanuts, exclaimed, 'Ports good.'

Then we moved to the sports' field.

I asked why the boys paused and looked upwards before participating in the running, broad jump and short dashes.

137

Gladys explained that Indian children believe that some Great Spirit guides them, and that when a boy approaches manhood each one has a guiding spirit, which is in the form of an animal or bird of which he has dreamed. She said, 'We have respect and fear for the bear, which may harm or help us, according to the way we approach it. The eagle is the most powerful.'

Peter paused, raised his eyes skyward and spurted forward. I wondered whether the bear, the eagle, or the powerful lion was Peter's guiding spirit. My guess was the majestic eagle.

Edgar and Elsie, Philip and Martha, Peter and Stella, lined up for the first couples in one of their favourite quick-change races. The boys carried suitcases containing outlandish, mission bale clothing. Each couple, hand in hand, raced to the marker, dumped the contents of the suitcases on to the ground, pulled on the odd clothing, and started back. Edgar, in one of those fifty-year-ago, full, red petticoats and an old lady's bonnet, with high heeled shoes, looked anything but feminine. Holding an umbrella over their heads, he and Elsie, dressed in a pair of men's trousers, shoes and coat, two or three sizes too large, topped by a derby hat, raced, neck to neck, with Philip and Martha. A couple of feet from the home base, Martha stepped on the cuff of her man's blue overall legs, tripped, and fell. Edgar and Elsie had won the race. Cheers went up from every throat, while Peter and Stella trailed in – like tortoises.

Umbrellas were practically never seen on Tokawaka reservation. Edgar, clad in a clowning costume, racing along in the hot sun, holding an umbrella was too ridiculous for even those stoical, hard-bitten faces. Wrinkled faces crinkled slowly into smiles. Even Skookum Johns and Skookum Thomas' customary grunts actually broke into laughter.

At the close of sports, the tired, hungry crowd squatted about the grass and gorged on cake, sandwiches, and lemonade, provided by the School. Freddie was in heaven. His eyes sparkling, with one hand cramming food into his mouth, the other rubbing his bulging stomach, he lisped, 'I's full. I's happy.'

Evening prayers, a few moments to undress, then lights out. It had been an unusually, exciting day. Little tots, bursting with excitement, just had to talk to someone. Separated from their parents, they had to be satisfied with forbidden whispering.

138

As familiar giggles and voices penetrated through the partitions, remembering our childhood parties, we felt justified in turning deaf ears, thus, we gave the children a little leeway.

'Jeannie's peculiar giggle, I would know it anywhere,' remarked Ellen.

' 'Opes we do it again. I's full!' Happy Freddie must have an elastic bread basket.

'I have never seen a child enjoy food as he did tonight,' said John.

'Sh-h-h, they will hear you. Go to sleep.' Motherly Martha.

A few more whispers before Martha and Stella settled down to pleasant dreams about the boys they had been allowed to play with during the day. Ordinarily boys and girls never mixed except in the class rooms.

Murmurs in the dormitories died away. I recalled Jeannie's plea, 'Let's play that game again.' It was after her first fire drill. Sports and fire drills, bright spots in her little life, were all the same to her, and to most of the children.

I dropped off into dreamland.

139

CHAPTER 15

CHRISTMAS IN TOKAWAKA

Excitement everywhere! Every spare moment, the children practised for their Christmas concert. One particular afternoon, Ellen warned us to be quiet and then we tiptoed to the girls' work-room where they were sewing and singing an Indian chorus. The tune, but not the words, seemed to be that of 'Good King Wenceslas'. When Stella spied us, the singing stopped immediately. Although Ellen begged them to continue, they refused to sing.

Martha explained that the words meant, 'Jesu your king is born, Jesus is born; in Excelsis gloria'. She said that Mrs King had taught them the words and the tune.

In answer to my questions, Mrs King said that she first heard this carol sung by an Indian girls' chorus on a reservation in Manitoba. Later, she learned that it is supposed to be the first Canadian Christmas carol, 'Twas in the moon of winter time when all the birds had fled.'

I searched for its source and discovered that a missionary, Jean de Brebeuf, working among the Indians, composed this carol for his Huron converts. He used ideas and words familiar to these new Christians. The words were passed on to their descendants. In 1926, a poet J. E. Middleton, translated the words into English and a Canadian musician, Dr Healy Willan, wrote the music, which the girls were singing. In the carol the chiefs, from afar, present gifts to the Holy Family in a partially destroyed bark lodge. Instead of gold, frankincense, and myrrh, the gifts are beaver and fox furs.

In 1955, the officials of the National Museum chose this three hundred year old carol from a large collection of Indian songs, for the subject of an artistic drama on display.

While the children were practising for their concert, influenza struck the village. In a week School would close for the holidays. I knew that I would never be able to nurse all the children in the village. So to hasten recoveries, I moved the sickest, small children into the hospital rooms off my bedroom. Dormitories sounded like cough factories. Children with burning bodies, aching limbs, and running noses tossed about their cots. It was impossible to give much individual nursing care.

In the village, young and old curled up, like flies before insecticides, on the floor. Old Indians with insufficient nourishment or warm clothing did not expect nursing care. They simply curled up on cedar mats on the draughty floors. Babies whined in cradles. Middle aged women and men dragged about, trying to find food and warmth for their little ones.

It was impossible for one nurse to give all the patients proper care, so I approached Mr King regarding emergency provisions. He exclaimed, 'No use asking Mr Brant for extra help. There is no money allotted for such emergencies.'

I caught winks of sleep whenever possible, gave the sick aspirin tablets, cough syrup, and laxatives, a minimum amount of sympathy and comforting words, and trusted that Providence would do the rest.

Eventually School closed. The afternoon that the teachers and Mrs Grimsby left for Victoria for their Christmas holidays Mr King said that all children – sick and well – must be sent to their homes. Mrs King and he were entitled to holidays free from Indians and wanted to be with their children. They certainly needed a change, but it was with a sad heart that I saw half-sick children, with high fevers, drag themselves along the boardwalk in the cold rain, to homes containing sicker people, with no one to give them much, if any, care.

That night Mr King, in an apologetic voice, informed me that it was too expensive to keep the School heated for one nurse. He gave me an electric plate for my bedroom. I asked him if officials would approve of sick patients coming to the unheated dispensary for examinations and medicines, for physically and financially in the long run it would probably be more expensive. He shrugged his shoulders and replied, 'Can't go over Mr Brant's head. He must show a good financial report.'

He was helpless; the Indians as usual were the chief victims. This was the King's first Christmas in a real home. Their eldest

141

son would be away the next year, and they had every reason for making the break. Nonetheless I was surprised and somewhat vexed when he said that he was taking Mrs Blakeley, the School cook, to do the cooking for the family so that Mrs King could have a complete rest.

A gremlin whispered to me, 'Can he do this? You are engaged by the Mission and entitled to have meals, room, and heat provided.' Although stout-hearted, I was tired from the long physical and mental strain, and the thought of what was ahead of me, alone in that huge, draughty, barn-like building, made a wave of self pity sweep over me. I wept, for the temptation was strong. The boat would soon leave for Victoria. Why should I not go and enjoy a holiday like the rest of the staff? But a good angel whispered, 'You're a nurse. Stick to your post.'

At times I regretted that I had not followed the advice of the gremlin, although I was glad that I had remained, for not an Indian died.

I shall never forget that Christmas. With a sad heart, I wrapped myself in my old goat coat and mittens and attempted to pack a few boxes of cheer for some of the sick people in the village. My heart was not in the Christmas spirit mood. It rebelled against penny-pinching saving expenses for an extravagant government and church officials.

Christmas week unfortunately was bitterly cold and the penetrating rain and dampness, so familiar to that part of the Coast, added to the chilliness. It ate through the marrow of my bones. The small electric plate never seemed to warm my bedroom. The dispensary was cold and damp, and my clothes never thoroughly dry. Each night I dragged myself home from the village, tired and starving, but I lacked the energy to eat proper food. I crawled into bed, fully clothed, with extra sweaters and woollens, socks and a hot water bottle. Several times I had to make emergency night calls in the village. All the time my conscience was rebelling against my treatment. But my misguided conscience or foolish stubborn Scottish pride in the nursing profession, held me with the sick people.

A few sunny days helped clear up the village influenza before the children and staff returned to the School. But with the added mental strain, exhausted after battling single-handed with so many sick patients, I contracted acute bronchitis. I discovered that I was running a high temperature and unable to throw off an almost constant cough. I knew it would be foolish and asking for trouble to work among so many tubercular patients without having a few days' rest. I had also been warned to keep physically fit.

Regulations demanded that a nurse, even to take a full day's rest, must wire Toronto officials for consent. I wired the secretary. She informed me that, even with a temperature of 103 and a persistent cough, I was not justified in asking for a few days' leave and rest, without a doctor's certificate.

Too sick to care whether I lived or died, I shivered and perspired as I staggered in the cold rain over the half mile of slippery walk, then waded through the muddy village to the wharf. Lying on the board bunk, seasick and retching, I knew why something had prompted me on that hot August day to bring my old goat coat. Friends had kidded me about going to the North Pole. But it prevented me from contracting pneumonia and no doubt saved my life.

As I listened to the tremendous combers breaking against the sides of the boat, I felt part of the flying water. When water streamed aft across the deck, self pity uppermost, I did not feel the least bit heroic. My mind was past the state of registering sensations of beauty, might or power. We docked at the wharf, and I managed to climb up the ladder, then my legs went rubbery. Tender-hearted Bill slid his hand under my elbow and practically carried me up the long, icy hill to the doctor's office.

Dr Provost took one look, and said, 'You should have been in bed long ago. Don't you know better than to come out in such weather. You are like to get your death of cold. Take the next steamer to Victoria and go to bed. I will wire Toronto officials.'

I have little recollection of that rough homeward trip. The next day I went aboard the steamer without a guilty conscience. The kind-hearted stewardess on the S.S. *Norah* insisted that I stay in my berth. She returned with a mug of steaming broth and a delicious piece of fish. I had time to realize that there are two types of Christians; stained glass window ones, and unsung practising people. She was one of the latter.

143

Three days later, I removed my heavy clothing for the first time in three weeks, snuggled into a warm bed in a boarding house and slept the clock around.

I was well aware but for my stubborn pride this break might have been avoided. I had to learn the costly way. But I resolved then and there that never again would I let foolish pride in my profession overrule common sense. Between sleeping and eating, I had much time to meditate. The advice of my old instructress kept running through my mind: 'Always remember that you are not the only cog in a wheel. Long after you are dead and gone there will be more capable nurses to carry on.'

I might be only one small pebble dropped into a vast and limitless sea of humans, but I felt that I was doing a worthwhile thing and hoping that I was doing it well. Even if others might consider me foolish I felt well rewarded when I thought I was doing what I was meant to do.

My mind was torn between two thoughts. What was the use of returning to the reservation? There was no one to back me up and I was getting nowhere. My conscience kept pricking. 'Go back, the Indians need you.' I had become fond of the papooses and many of the adults, understood some of their problems, and they were beginning to trust and confide in me. My mulish nature to make good, or desire to meet their needs, predominated. I returned, but with a determination to spend the rest of my term working for the interest of Indians, regardless of consequences.

The Victoria doctor gave me a first-class, medical report, and I started back to Tokawaka.

This time when I stepped off the *Norah,* I lacked that spontaneous enthusiasm to fulfil childhood dreams, which had inspired me on my first trip up the Coast, and which had upheld me during the past few months.

CHAPTER 16

THE REFUGEES

I had taken it for granted that John Mark's head was normal, until Gladys informed me that when a prince is born he has to have his head bound to make it grow to the shape desired by his father. It seemed almost incredible that parents in North America, in this day and age, would bind babies' heads even to make beautiful-shaped skulls. At the next community meeting, I took particular pains to explain to the mothers the bad effect of this custom. They sat silent and passive. I realized that persuasion or argument would be useless to influence them to abandon such an ancient practice. But should I or someone else instil the thought in their mind that such a practice was useless and bad for the child they might abandon the custom gradually, so I pegged away tactfully, setting the ball rolling for my successor. But one never knows what goes on in an Indian's brain. My suggestions may still be digging away through their brains, and some day they may bore deep enough to have some effect.

Skookum Thomas declared that he could tell the morrow's weather by the way the wind blew, by the way the snow fell down, and by the way smoke spirals. His barometer was much more reliable than some of our radio weather reporters and newspapers. I soon learned to use my own eyes, my nose and my ears, and hoped that some day I might even be able to forecast storms correctly.

In order to survive, Indians had to be skilful hunters, using meagre resources to great purpose. Characteristics have been passed down through generations until today no Indian rushes into anything. Every act is deliberated, whether he hitches his trousers, ties his snowshoes, carves a totem pole, tracks game, or makes shelter. 'The longest way round is the shortest way home,' sums up Indian philosophy admirably.

K   145

We soon learned that Indians like animals, seemed to know to the fraction of an inch how much space there was along a ledge, and how small a log would bear their weight safely over two hundred feet of rushing water. They could sense dangerous ice holes in quagmires, and could smell the foul weather and danger. Patience was one of their qualities, and they thought of time only in terms of useful effort. In the non-Indian sense, saving and work are ludicrous to them. Not slaves to minutes or hours, they never let time tell them what to do, and when to do a thing. The thing that counted was not in days or hours, but what happened at various seasons of the year. Time was snow, downpour of rain, day of spring, mosquitoes, blackflies, spells of weather, feasts and lean periods, forest fires, fish runs, or the day the ice went out.

We should bear in mind that many non-Indians never try to understand the fact that the essence of an Indian's life is to be; not to become something he is not.

March came in like a lion. I turned on the radio just as the speaker was announcing, 'Indian School burned to the ground. No lives lost. Children have been taken into homes for the night.'

The following morning a wire came saying, 'Boat on way bringing seven children who have no homes.'

Two evenings later after dark, Mr Brant and seven drenched children came streaking up the boardwalk, in a freezing rain and biting wind. Their teeth chattering, they were blue and shivering. Water streamed from their clothes, slocked on to the floor and squashed from their canvas shoes. Stripped of water-logged clothing, they eagerly ate huge slices of bread, peanut butter, and drank steaming cocoa.

Wilfred, Tommy, Joe, Bill, Noah, and two sisters, Aggie and Mary, had features quite different to our School children. My attention was arrested by the girls' round, soft, blue eyes, fair complexions, and flaxen hair. Somewhere someone had been left to bring them up alone I thought what a heritage these children had – no home, and not wanted.

My eyes were magnetically drawn to nine year old Aggie. Slumped on the bench, making a desperate effort to sit up straight, her hand was shaking so badly she could hardly hold

146

her cup of cocoa. Every few moments she rested her head on her hand, coughed deeply, wiped something from her mouth and looked up to see if anyone noticed her. Anyone with any intelligence could guess what was causing that cough and expectorating. Tell-tale pink wiped on to the back of her hands; two bright red spots, like burning embers, under her feverish eyes, in her peeked face, spindly legs, were all symptoms of active tuberculosis.

In the dispensary I discovered that Aggie had a temperature of 102 , It seemed incredible that any doctor, nurse, principal, or agent, all of which were available for Aggie's reservation and School, would send this dying tubercular child on such a trip, to be admitted into a School with seventy children. I reported my diagnosis to Mr King, and stood firm in my refusal to allow Aggie to be admitted into the School dormitories until a doctor could make a diagnosis. I hated to separate these two lonely mites, but in the overcrowded dormitories with so many children I could not endanger the health of all.

Aggie was glad to go to the hospital ward. She sipped another cup of cocoa while I packed her in hot water bottles. Then she gave a wan, appreciative smile, sank back on to her pillows and went sound asleep. In the morning hard-squeezed, blood-stained wads of tissue scattered about the bed were evidence of a correct diagnosis.

Mr Brant informed us that Mary's and Aggie's mother was dying with tuberculosis; that no white home was open to these children, and there was no other place on the reservation for them. The doctor, principal, and nurse had declared that they were too busy to give individual attention, nor had they noticed that Aggie was sick. This passing of the buck was too much for me. Seventy children and the staff in a closely packed School could not be unnecessarily exposed to such deadly infection.

I wired Dr Provost, who replied, 'Mr Brant is responsible for finding a place for Aggie in her own district. Send her back to him.' It was easy to give instructions to send Aggie back, but more difficult to send this dying child miles down the Coast alone. But although cruel, with so many lives in our hands it had to be done.

Mr King agreed that we should send her back, but he said,

'The problem is to find someone to keep an eye on her while she is on the S.S. *Norah*. I definitely will not send such a sick child back in an open boat. And it would be tragic if the captain reported finding a dead Indian child alone in the hatch.' [Segregation rules stipulated Indians in the hatch.]

John exclaimed, 'Good for Mr King!'

Once again Providence intervened. The next day, Gladys introduced me to Mrs Buick, who was going down on the S.S. *Norah* to Aggie's reservation. She volunteered to care for her and see her safely to Mr Brant's secretary. But even then there was difficulties. Mr King said: 'I am willing to have Aggie carried to the School boat, but a stretcher patient will arouse suspicion and require too much explanation. The purser will never accept a dying Indian child, especially with tuberculosis. I hate to ask Aggie to walk, but I can't think of any alternative. We will hide the stretcher on our boat and let her walk aboard.'

With only a few days or weeks to live, walking would not do Aggie much harm. But would she be able to walk that far without staggering. Indian children have an unlimited amount of will power on which to draw and they give up only when their last ounce of strength is gone. I gave her a strong stimulant, and sick as she was she seemed to sense the necessity of putting up a brave front. At ten o'clock, that cold, March morning, I took one hand, Mrs Buick the other, and Aggie walked spryly up the gang-plank. I made her as comfortable as possible, gave her a handful of candy and wrapped her in a blanket. Her eyes brightened, she smiled faintly, waved good-bye, and I went back to work with a heavy heart.

All that day, a picture of that wee, pathetic face kept haunting my mind. I wondered if any of the officials would allow one of their children to receive such treatment. I never heard from Aggie, but not long afterwards a sanatorium for tubercular patients was built on the West Coast. If it were instigated indirectly by such patients as Aggie, her life may not have been sacrified in vain. Had Aggie lived today she would have been sent to this Indian sanatorium.

On Thursday I took the other six children across to Dr Provost. It was Freddie's birthday, a great event for him, so he was allowed to accompany us. When we left the School at eight o'clock, it was an ideal morning. We crept along the white, frosted walk to the wharf, and went aboard the *Daybreak*. The invigorating salt breeze put a zip in the air and snapped the children awake.

Bill guided the boat out into the channel, and exclaimed, 'For once, it looks as though we might have a lovely trip across!'

The hot sun beat down, delightfully warm, on the grey, canvas-covered deck. The children, old enough not to fall overboard, stayed out on deck, wound the quilts around their bodies, Indian fashion. They curled up on the raised hatch door, and basked in the sun's rays, like seals.

Mary, shy by nature or from having been knocked about from pillar to post, snuggled close, looked up into my face and whispered, 'This is fun.' Such words spoken by an Indian child meant a lot. Away from restricted freedom she could be her natural self and relax.

Most of the children of mixed blood were more restless and wriggly than full-blood Indian children. They could not sit silent for long periods, like the full-blood children.

Mary wiggled about and chatted. 'The Great Spirit is taking my mother home. I have two brothers and a little sister. They never let Aggie and I go home from the other School, because my mother has a bad germ, which we might catch. I hardly remember what Lily, that's my baby sister, looks like. She must be a very, big girl now. And I know my mother misses me because she used to hold me in her lap.' She snuggled close, so I took her on to my lap, and asked her if she was lonesome without Aggie. She replied, 'Oh, some, but I didn't see much of her at the other School. She was always coughing and could not play with us. But she tried to hide her cough from the nurse and from Mr Monk. He was our principal. But I do like Jeannie and Beatrice. We play together here.'

In the few short hours Mary had been at the School, she had adjusted herself to her new surroundings and had made friends with at least two girls.

The surface of the glassy water was exceptionally changeable for that time of the year; wonderful, vivid green, transparent, shimmering, under the sun's silvery rays, then rippling with the gentle breeze. The boat left a wide foamy wake. Fluffy and

round bubble clouds bounced together overhead. Two screaming, murky-white gulls followed the boat, coaxing for a handout.
The water was never five minutes the same, shifting to mixtures
of blues, greens, and amethyst.

Stunted furze clung to the steep cliffs on the rocky shores,
mingling with green-brown patches of rocks and moss, which
merged into a mass of early saffron, wild flowers. An exquisite
picture. It was great to be alive and gliding over the restful water.
Peace and relaxation replaced the hubbub of routine and
regular School life. Too soon we docked at the wharf and went
up the hill to Dr Provost's office.

The weather and face of the channel, on this part of the
Coast, can change as suddenly and as fiercely as the mind of a
perverse woman. At three o'clock when the doctor finished
examining the children, falling, sleety rain made little tapping
noises on the walk, then there was a feeling of snow in the
air. Occasional zigzags of lightning cut the coal-black vault of
threatening sky, shooting swords and spears. The sun had disappeared and the wind, increasing in force, blew across our faces.
Gulls cut capers, like crazy birds, before the pending storm.
Foamy white caps, far out across the water, rode shoreward,
spelling dirty weather.

Bill headed the boat homeward, and exclaimed, 'We are in
for it! 'Twill be a rough trip, but there is no alternative. We
have to get the children home tonight.'

The boat, bucking each oncoming, powerful wave, lurched
forward and sideways, reeling drunkenly through the mad water.
Salt spray spewed in all directions showering the deck with icy
brine. The children and I huddled together in the cabin. Mary
tired and sleepy, cuddled under a blanket on my lap, and I kept
Wilfred, Freddie, and Joe close beside me – the only way to
protect small children from being thrown about the cabin. The
older boys, accustomed to rough water, had to fend for themselves. Again, the results of mixed blood were displayed. Full-
blood Indians as a rule are good sailors. But Mary was retching
and vomiting. I held her over the emergency bucket until a
terrific wave struck the boat broadside. Then I gulped,
swallowed hard, leaned over and lost my dinner.

The awful impact of the wave on the boat threw Joe to the

floor. His head struck the side of the bench. Tommy picked him up, plunked him firmly on the bench, wiped off the blood, with his coat sleeve, and comforted him, saying, 'That's nothing. I've been on the water when the boat fairly stood on end. What's a little cut?'

In an effort to be a young brave, Joe stopped whimpering, Mary's heaving stomach took a breathing spell, I swallowed a few more oozy gulps, the boat righted itself, then plunged forward into the fast-gathering storm. Every moment the sea grew more crazy and powerful. The damp air penetrated through the quilts and bit to the marrow of our bones. Although the night was ebony black, Bill managed to steer it straight as it ploughed through the churning water to the village wharf.

I have a nightmarish recollection of that last pitching hour of the trip, and I remember vividly mooching behind Tommy's swinging flashlight, sheltering Mary under my raincoat, splashing through the mud puddles, as we skidded and crawled along the slippery boardwalk. At eight o'clock, we stumbled into the warm School, chilled and drenched to the skin. Another of March's lion days had ended.

Dr Provost had told me that he would be over on Saturday to remove Lucy's and Lena's tonsils, so we changed the dispensary into an operating room. Saturday was another nightmarish day, which I would not like to repeat. Lucy and Lena, fully conscious, sat upright in a chair in front of the doctor, while he fumbled around and took out tonsils and adenoids. I helped the children stagger upstairs to their dormitory beds, placed side by side, As it was necessary to get some sleep, I had to trust to Providence. We tucked the children into beds near the door and instructed Martha to call me if she heard them crying. They slept the night through.

CHAPTER 17

QUINK

Saturday evening, when John Mark returned to the School, I noticed a bulge under his coat. He edged his way past Mrs King, who was on duty, and dodged behind an older boy. I knew he was smuggling some treasure up to the dormitory to add to his precious hoard. By strategy, he reached the back stairs and sneaked up to the dormitory, forbidden territory during the day.

John Mark knew that Mrs King would miss him and come up to see why he had disobeyed the rules of the School. He knew also that she had a tender heart and hoped that he might coax her into letting him keep his treasure, a baby seal left stranded when John Mark's grandfather, Skookum Jacobson, had shot its mother on a sealing expedition. Later I learned that when Skookum Jacobson saw the newly born seal, the spark of human tenderness so often encountered with these Indians, caused tears to trickle down his cheeks. He could not leave that wee seal with its human-like face and pitiful whine to starve to death. But he had not the heart to shoot such a helpless animal, so he lifted it carefully, put it into his coat pocket. Then he was faced with the problem of what to do with the tiny animal. He knew the ruthlessness of so many boys together, and also that the School regulations forbade live pets. His wife was dead and he had to return to the sealing waters the following Monday. John Mark saw the seal and coaxed so hard to be allowed to keep it and take it to the School for his own pet that his grandfather with many misgivings gave his consent.

John Mark needed someone or something to pour out his affection on. His mother had died when he was very young; his grandmother a few years later. His cunning brain must think of some means to forestall a deserved scolding for breaking rules. He must make Mrs King love that seal and let him keep it. Like

152

most Indians he had great insight, and knew that underneath her forbidding frowns there must be a soft heart which he might be able to touch.

When the children were settled, Mrs King told me how he had won the day. She said, 'I opened my mouth to scold him but he stepped forward and actually thrust that seal into my arms before I could say a word. I am not exaggerating when I say that seal seemed to know what it was all about. Its tiny whiskers twitched. A large tear oozed down its cheek, and those pleading eyes looked straight into mine. And instead of scolding him, I said, 'John Mark, *where* did you get that seal?'

' "Oh, Mrs King, he is so helpless, grandfather killed his mother yesterday, and he heard the Great Spirit say, 'Indian, you have killed the mother, you must care for the baby.' You know grandfather lives alone and has to go out sealing Monday. There is no one to feed the seal. It will die. You tell us in Sunday School that we must love all dumb animals. Can't I keep him here? We will take care of him. He will not eat much. If you think it costs too much to feed him, Freddie and Paul said they would go without their milk. Freddie is so lonesome with no one to play with him. Oh, Mrs King, please, we do so want to have a live pet," pleaded John Mark.

'An icicle would have melted before his pleading. I handed the seal back to him, but warned him. "If I ever see anyone abusing or neglecting to feed this seal, I will take it away immediately."

' "Thank you, thank you, Mrs King. We will take good care of it" promised John Mark.

'Even the seal's wee face wrinkled its nose and its eyes peered at me as much as to express its appreciation. I can't exactly say that tenderness and love shone from its eyes, but that is what John Mark saw. I have never seen his face look so happy. Guessing that he was planning to take the seal to bed with him, although I hated to disappoint him, I told him; "John Mark, that seal cannot live in the dormitory."

'A disappointed expression flitted over his face, as he replied, "No, Mrs King."

'You may go now and you have my permission to take Freddie and Paul out to build him a little house. I will ask Nurse for a bottle and a nipple. When you have finished his home, I will give you some warm milk.'

I saw his radiant face, as clasping his little pet to his heart, he raced down the stairs, out to the playground to share his pride and joy with the other children. Curious to see the seal, I went outside, where John and Ellen, surrounded by seventy eager expectant children had their whole attention focused on one wee animal. John, kneeling in a squatting position, his buttocks resting on his heels, his hand gently but firmly grasping the seal's neck. As I arrived, the seal tilted its head slightly upwards and forward to a forty-five degree angle. Ellen, the nursing bottle in her left hand, prised its mouth open wide enough to slip the nipple into it. As she gave the bottle an extra push forward, the seal made a quick movement, jerked its head sideways and wiggled away. The nipple skidded upward and a stream of milk squirted straight into John's eye. Everything happened so quickly, he jumped backwards to see what had struck him, overbalanced; to save himself, he loosened his hold on the seal. It rolled on to its flippers shook itself and flopped awkwardly towards John Mark. With snapping eyes, the children swayed forward into a smaller circle. John Mark picked up his seal and carried it back to John.

Eight-thirty, time to ring the prayer bell. John glanced at his watch and raised his eyes to Ellen, questioningly. I said : 'Suppose we risk it?' So we went on with our efforts.

We could not disappoint those eager happy children, and they could not leave that seal hungry. Ellen nodding agreement, raised the baby's head again and pushed open its mouth. Instinct, hunger pains, or a sense of what was expected of him, made it open its mouth, clamp its gums firmly about the nipple and start to suck. Their faces glowing and eyes sparkling, the children wiggled their bodies closer to the seal.

Loath to give up its soother until the last drop of milk was extracted from the bottle, there was no stopping that seal. Eventually, it rolled over on to its flippers. John Mark gathered his sleeping pet into his arms, and with Freddie and Paul following him carried the bulging animal down to the shore, where they tucked it into its little bed made of grass and leaves, beside a tiny pool of salt water, which Paul had carried from the water's edge in an old tin can. He had insisted that seals had to have salt water in which to wash themselves and to keep cool, but not enough for them to get drowned.

Fortunately for all, Mr King was still in the village. No one was any the wiser that prayers commenced twenty minutes late. All had enjoyed the extra freedom, and perhaps it had been more educational than an extra few minutes of algebra, or more valuable than the amount of time spent in routine compulsory prayer.

The next day, the moment the children were dismissed for lunch hour, John Mark approached John, and said, 'You know seals have to have exercise in salt water. We should put him into the water before he has his dinner.' Granted permission, he ran up to the dormitory and came back in a jiffy clad in bathing trunks. When I arrived on the scene the children were squatting or hunched up on the sand and rocks, eagerly looking forward to the seal's first swim.

John Mark exclaimed, 'You know if I put him in from the shore, he may swim out to sea and be drowned.' We thought this somewhat optimistic, but bowed to his judgement!

He waded out three feet and gently lowered the seal under water. Before he raised his hands, its miniature flippers made quick, short strokes forward, which grew stronger and faster. In a few seconds, the seal was back on the shore shaking its flippers and whisking the water from its nose and whiskers. Its wee face looked up as much as to say, 'That's the life! Didn't I do that well?'

John Mark took it out again. Once more it popped up on shore and flipped about.

'He learn quinck! Let's call him Quink!' shouted Freddie. Although he was putting sentences together, his English was far from perfect, especially when he was excited. But from then on, during his short life, Quink was the seal's name.

Quink received the devoted attention of the children, and often that of the staff, especially John. In a week's time it became a spoiled baby. Then one morning before breakfast, with a woebegone face, John Mark told us that Quink was dead.

His voice had tears in it as he asked, 'Why did Quink die?', but true to tradition, he would not let himself shed tears. I

155

assured him that it was not his fault, that he had taken good care of his pet, but that it was not the seal's natural home. Without its mother, on land and all alone, it just could not live, so its Great Spirit had taken it home to care for it. This thought seemed to give him some comfort.

After breakfast Freddie, Jeannie and Paul with solemn faces came to the dispensary, and Jeannie said, 'Mrs Grimsby give permission funeral.' Freddie added, 'Bury Quink back School.' Jeannie continued, 'Nurse, come say words Quink go Great Spirit.' But there was no customary wailing – Quink had a Christian funeral.

Each morning, a few wild flowers were laid on the tiny grave. Every time the children thought about their pet their usually merry faces had sad expressions. Then their short memories forgot about him, with only an occasional whisper of 'Poor Quink,' from Freddie.

CHAPTER 18

THE SALE

I had learned that the dole system, or any system where everything is handed out, has a tendency to take away initiative and lessen value of property received. People on the receiving end over a period of time become reluctant to stand on their own feet.

This was happening with some Tokawaka women. Ellen and I agreed that they had been handed things too long without being asked to give anything in return, and that they would be far happier if they could be shown and helped to a more independent way of living.

The mothers and grandmothers were pleased with the idea of an objective – sewing for an Easter sale. We agreed that money earned by their own self-labour give them more satisfaction than something merely handed to them. We decided with or without Mr King's permission it would give them a chance to help themselves.

Eaton's and Simpson's stores gave generously of free material for a nucleus to start the new undertaking. Friends and relatives sent us odds and ends of material. Once interested the women were eager and willing to work hard. Each week they came to the community house. At first this adventure was too new for these taciturn women to contribute much to the social hour. They were good listeners while I carried on a one-sided monologue. The older women, knowing that I did not understand Indian, soon began to chatter like monkeys. The ones who understood and spoke English gradually joined in the conversation.

I learned much more about their intimate and immediate interests and problems during these meetings than I would have done merely by visiting in the homes. I got an inkling of how they felt concerning their children being taken away from them,

157

and their attitude to the School and staff. It gave me an insight
into their home surroundings, what they thought about the treatment by the government, and the problems their chiefs faced.

No baby sitters were needed for these mothers. They came
with babies spreadeagled on their shoulders and with one or two
toddling youngsters. The small tots crawled about, playing with
toys, sucking candy and strewing sandwich crumbs about the
floor. When a stomach demanded more satisfying food, a
mother hauled up her child, plopped it on to her broad lap,
flipped down the front of her dress. The baby nuzzled against
her soft bosom, like a fuzzy puppy, as it gulped down life-saving
milk, When satisfied, the baby continued to play with toys or
curled up on the floor and slept.

Each week, the women counted their articles and watched
the pile of homework growing. One day Gladys informed me,
'They want to know can't we have the sale next week?'

On sale day, I was pleased to note their intense joy, tinged
with a feeling of responsibility for the anticipated and much
talked-about sale. Women popped their heads out of homes,
and asked, 'What time does it start?' No matter what time I
said, they would be there an hour or so ahead of me.

These Indian women were not fitted by nature for com-
petition, neither did they have any desire to grasp power. Whatever they possessed was worth only its exact immediate useful-
ness. They could sit for hours in anticipation of an event, simply
for its enjoyment, or with full stomachs they could bask in delightful laziness and contentment.

Men, women, and children were squatting on the grass and
steps, waiting for me to pronounce the sale open for business.
I unlocked the door and they swarmed like bees into a hive into
the community house. Although this was their first sale, the
women, as if from frequent habit, took their chosen places behind the long tables of clothing. They had participated,
anticipated, and now they partook. Articles were held up, tried
on, squeezed, discussed, and bought. A much more interesting
and fascinating event than a nine o'clock, city basement sale.

About half of the articles had been sold when Mr King called
me aside and said, 'Jake wants to get married right away.' The
previous month, honest, simple-minded Jake, a widower and

158

the church janitor, returned from another reservation with a woman for a wife. Mr King had frequently warned him that if he wished to hold his position as janitor of a Christian church he must marry Judith at a Christian wedding or not live with her. Every time he replied, 'She not yet decided if she want me.'

But something had made him come to a sudden decision, and he sought Mr King and said, 'She marry me this afternoon.'

As Judith had not professed Christianity, Mr King came to ask if I would close the sale for an hour before she had a chance to change her mind. A wedding like a baptism was an event. We closed the doors of the community house, School was dismissed, Jake ran the church bell and everyone drifted over to the church.

It was not necessary to set the hour. By some peculiar grapevine system, the whole village knew that when the bell ceased to ring Jake's wedding would start. The last peal of the bell died away as we arrived at the church, packed with men, women, children, with dogs looking through the door. Mr King kept Jake and his bride close to him, lest they change their minds and vanish.

As Judith did not speak or understand English, Mr King had asked fifteen year old Lucy to stand as interpreter for this elderly couple. When everyone was seated, Jake and Judith went to the altar where Mr King was pacing back and forth. Lucy was nowhere to be seen. Eventually he motioned for the audience to sit. Jake said something to Judith. She put her hand over her mouth and snickered. I would have given a month's salary to know what Jake told his bride that produced such a quick change in her mask-like face. After much whispering and head nodding among the girls, Stella stood up, and announced, 'Please, Mr King, Lucy has gone to the School to get her new red sweater.'

Lucy having acquired the white girls' desire of vanity, had persuaded Ellen to go with her to get her birthday sweater, a gift from her mother. Ten minutes later, wearing her red sweater and beret, she marched proudly up the aisle to the front of the church. Mr King motioned to Jake and Judith. They strolled back to the altar and stood beside Lucy. Mr King waited until they were reasonably adjusted. Then, in a solemn voice, he read, 'Jake, do you take Judith Sail to be your wife? To look after when she is sick and when she grows old.'

'I do,' replied Jake.

Mr King turned to Lucy, and said, 'Ask Judith if she will take Jake to be her husband. If she will promise to look after him when he is sick and when he grows old. Ask her if she will live with him only and not with any other man?'

Judith and Lucy chatted together in Indian until Judith appeared satisfied with the nature of the obligations of a Christian marriage. She nodded her consent and Lucy replied to Mr King: 'Judith says she will stay with him always until he goes to his Great Spirit.'

Mr King could only assume that Judith understood his conditions and that Lucy had interpreted his questions and answers correctly.

I suddenly remembered an incident which happened many years before when the Mounted Police had to interpret through their scout Jerry noted for his terse and taciturn ways. The Mountie had to listen to an hour-long oration from the chief on how his people had benefited from police protection. Then Jerry interpreted the grandiose speech with one short sentence, 'He say him damn glad.'

The ritual over, Jake and Judith drew long sighs, scuffed down the aisle, went through the door and stood waiting for the people to come out. Mr King had pronounced the benediction in English, which they had heard so often that many of them recognized but did not understand. But he was not able to congratulate the bride, because she did not speak English, Nevertheless his and the congregation's handshakes and smiles showed Judith that she was now properly married according to Christian custom, and welcomed into the community.

John remarked, 'What a strange wedding; no ring exchange, bridesmaids best man, or rice throwing! Rather a nice way! Guess I'll be married Indian fashion!'

Jake and Judith's honeymoon consisted of ducking into the low door of his one-room shack back of the church, where they had been living for several weeks.

The next morning, Little Benny stopped me, and said, 'Mum, say ask Nurse, 'nother sale, soon?'

160

In spite of the wedding interruption, we considered the sale a social and financial success.

All one Saturday night rain beat against the building, but Sunday morning dawned bright and clear. The children lined up to march to church. Old man's whiskers' moss on the sodden planks of the boardwalk resembled slimy rocks. Agile as mountain goats, the children did not have any difficulty keeping their feet, but the staff skidded about the narrow boards. Half-way through the woods, Jeannie stopped suddenly, pointed to a tall tree and exclaimed, 'Look, see, squirrel head down!'

Ellen looked up one second too long. Her feet shot from under her and she plunged five feet below, striking her head on a sharp stump. By the time John and I lowered ourselves over the edge of the boards, blood gushed from a two-inch, jagged, scalp wound. We helped her back to the School, badly shaken and bruised. As there is always danger of infection or concussion with a skull wound, I advised her to go across to Dr Provost, but she did not feel equal to making the long trip, so I drew the gash together with adhesive tape. Although much concerned about their teacher's head, the children enjoyed this recess from classes. Frequently one of them would knock at the door and ask, 'She's not going to die, is she?'

Ellen still carries a large, jagged scar to remind her of that famous boardwalk.

Another Saturday the sun burst forth. Buds were swelling on the trees. The smell of spring and forest brought nostalgic homesickness. An unsettled urge jittered our spirits. The three of us were free for the afternoon and evening. When we left the dining-room, John said, 'This may be the last time that the three of us will be free at the same time before we separate at the end of the term. The boys have been telling me tales about a wonderful sunny sandy beach, four miles beyond the thicket. But Philip said the trail is very rough. What do you think?'

Ellen and I were beginning to feel like the children confined and stifled – with a desire to get away from Indians for a few hours. Should there be a real emergency, Mrs Grimsby agreed to send an Indian boy, who could reach us in a short time.

So leaving the School far behind, we pushed aside overhanging bushes – still dripping cold dew – and climbed up and under fallen logs and underbrush. Soon the intense, pure air and the open spaces put new life into us. It was so quiet and peaceful one could have heard a pin fall. Golden shafts of sunshine penetrated through the azure sky. Budding wild flowers pushed their perky heads through the damp earth, as if they too felt the spring life. The vivid smell of cedar and furze penetrated our nostrils. The day seemed carved to meet our needs. The clouds climbed higher, and our spirits soared upward.

John pushed back the last half-opened leaves and low bushes. It was like stepping into fairy-land. A magnificent panorama of sky, sea and white sand confronted us. Hundreds of feet of soft white sand carpeted the beach. The tide had ebbed, leaving the shore high and dry. An intense heat for this time of the year beat down on the sand. Waves gently lapped the pebbles. The delicious tart twang of salt air filled our nostrils, and waves rippled as they lapped shoreward. We stood gazing seaward across the interminable miles of blue-green, watery expanse. Tempting water made us scurry behind bushes, change into bathing suits, and enjoy the delightful feeling of bare feet on sand. Carefree, we ran over the hot sand to the water's edge, and without waiting to dread the first, cold plunge, waded in, and let the receding sand ooze slowly between our toes. What bliss! We swam out and rode back on the incoming tide until our bodies tingled and glowed, Then we stretched full length, like rabbits, on the warm sandy cushion. Like the Indians the rest of the world did not exist – we lived for the moment.

Although we made the most of every moment of the afternoon under the changing sky with its marshmallow, scudding clouds, too soon the sun's rays shortened and the air blew cold across the sea.

John looked at the sky, and remarked, 'I don't like the look of the clouds. But I don't think I can resist one last dip. Coming?'

Afterwards, we scouted about and collected driftwood, smooth as sandpapered boards, hung a pail on two sticks between two stones, in a sheltered corner, and threw in twigs to settle the ashes. We sat drinking boiled tea until goose pimples sprouted on our bodies. With stomachs full of tea and sandwiches, a lazy, lethargic feeling crept over us. I had never seen anything as beautiful as that last glow of sunset.

'Let's stay just ten minutes more,' begged Ellen.

Gulls winnowed and screamed. Tiny sandpipers tripped daintily along the sand, making short, quick pecks at invisible insects.

Eventually we tore ourselves away and John asked, 'Shall we take the other trail home? Philip said it was much shorter, but harder to follow?'

We could not resist the challege of unknown paths and set off. A mile from the beach, traces led to another trail. Although the sun had gone, for the first mile, it was fairly easy to follow the beaten path. Then twilight set in and it became more and more difficult to push through the dark foliage to follow the almost invisible markings. Eventually the trail led to an opening and we faced black muck. John scouting ahead, stopped and shouted back, 'Do you see what I see? There is the log Philip said we would have to walk. He said, "There's black muck under it like quicksand. Keep to the log." '

A weather-worn, gnarled tree, covered with sharp limbs and slippery moss, two feet in diameter, spanned the twenty foot gap across muck and water. After studying the situation from all angles, John said, 'I will take you over one at a time. It is too late to return to the other trail.'

As I watched John and Ellen grasp the protruding limbs, swing forward, and crawl along the log, it looked so easy, my overconfident ego made me daring. I started, got half-way across and confidently swung from one limb to the next. My feet shot out from under me. Rip went my breeches and a firelike sear shot through my shin. Fortunately for me, the corduroy material held. There I gracefully dangled in mid-air above quicksand and muck, uttering a prayer that the cloth would hold until John could reach me.

He shouted, 'For the love of Mike, don't start walking by yourself again.'

I wondered how he thought I could walk with my feet and arms in space, my body dangling between sky and earth. He crawled slowly out to me, and together we reached the other side safely. I swabbed out the green-moss embedded in a deep skin wound, wiped away the trickling blood, tucked in a tissue and trusted to Providence to prevent infection setting in until I reached the dispensary. Like Ellen, I still carry a large branded V, which will ever remind me of Indians and that shorter trail. On account of my foolishness, we had lost much time and darkness had set in.

John remembered that Philip had said, 'Just before starting the last mile, there is a pile of stones at the edge of the underbrush. Once you find the stones, crawl through the hole among the overhanging bushes, duck under, find the trail, and it will lead you to the School.'

It had seemed so simple to Philip, but very difficult for John in the darkness to see stones or a hole in the bushes. Unfortunately we did not have the natural instinct of Indian boys. He volunteered to scout along the edge of the bushes, admonishing us not to leave the spot under any conditions. As he disappeared into the darkness, he shouted back, 'Don't try any more foolish stunts on your own. There may be a cougar around in the bushes.' He need say no more. We clung to each other with straining ears.

It seemed hours though it was only minutes before he shouted, and we joined him by a pile of stones. He pushed aside the bushes. Sure enough, we could distinguish the marks of a path. By bending almost double, we managed to crawl along under the low-hanging branches, until the dark outline of the School loomed ahead and guided us home.

We faced an irate principal. He could not understand why intelligent, grown-ups did such foolish things as explore unknown trails. 'Why didn't you tell me where you were going?'

John half-apologised, 'It was our free day. We could go wherever we pleased, and Mrs Grimsby, who was on duty, knew where we were.'

But after such an enjoyable afternoon, his temper affected us not a whit.

Instead of the customary fleas, papooses, and mechancial duties, I dreamed that night of sandy beaches, blue skies, salt air, and mincing sandpipers.

CHAPTER 19

GOODBYE TOKAWAKA

With everything so inconsistent in this reservation school, I had much sympathy for Indians. But I had a letter from our secretary saying that urgent need had arisen for a nurse to relieve in a New Canadian hospital for a year, and ended by saying 'We are transferring you at the end of the School year'.

I was not really sorry. Though I believed my work useful among the Indians, and had grown to appreciate their ways, I was tired of continually seeming to fight a single-handed battle.

I had merely been caught in the web, like other workers and the Indians. The only comfort was the thought that many more worthy persons than I had faced, and many more would face, similar situations. The full force of my nursing superintendent's warning came home to me, 'Do not compromise with injustice'. There were only a few weeks until the end of the term, so I accepted the offer and let the matter drop.

Days merged into each other as if on wings: complete examinations of each child; plasters and ointments for chronic sores; getting children ready to be released to the factories, advising parents before they left for the canneries.

Parents took their children to the canneries up the Coast. The men went out fishing, women and teenage girls worked in the canneries. Younger girls would care for the small children. Each year, mothers and children looked forward eagerly to this free life, away from compulsory routine, supervision and inspection. Although long, gruelling work hours in the canneries left little time to be with their children, mothers enjoyed working together and having their children with them in the evenings.

Class work ended on June 24th. The following day, Bill took John and Ellen by boat to Mucky Bay. Four of the children

165

and I went along to see them safely off on the small mail boat. Having lived and worked so closely together, enjoyed so many experiences together, and having discussed so many problems, we all felt part of each other's lives. As I waved farewell and watched their boat pass out of sight around the cliff, my eyes filled with tears. I felt as if I were waving away part of my life. There was only the promise of a reunion in Victoria to bolster me through the lonely and dispiriting days that followed.

During the next week I was very deeply touched by the plight of the Indians and by their little gifts, which they could ill afford – beaded serviette rings, reed vases, and carved eagles, treasures I would value for ever.

One day, Gladys' little Benny, beginning to speak a few English words, met me at the end of the boardwalk, as he frequently did, and handed me two white shells. He looked up at me, and said, 'Nurse go, miss Nurse.' His words touched me more than a dozen flowery farewell speeches.

Dan said, 'You stay, perhaps, I never drink again.'

Big John smiled, as he said, 'You stay, we pull well together.'

Freddie grinned, waved goodbye, and shouted, 'Good boy. Will blow nose always.'

I knew my time had not been wasted. I wished I could stay one more year but I would leave behind me life-long friends. Those stoical chiefs never forgot a kindness shown them. My interpreter, Nellie, and organist, Gladys, would remember me for awhile, but they would gradually forget. Should we ever meet, they would recall some little, long-forgotten incident, and would welcome me. These Indians seldom held a grudge – except against the government.

It had been one of the most difficult but most profitable, years of my life. I had made many blunders, had learned a lot about life in general, and had made many sincere friendships. I hoped that I had made a tiny dent in some brains behind those mask-like faces, which might have good results. If so, I would be satisfied with my year's work.

The last day of June, the steamer called. Mary, Wilfred, Tommy, Joe, and I climbed up the ladder and went aboard.

It was my job to see them safely to their parents or the agent. As Indians are not allowed to eat or sleep in the quarters used by white people, I found a place below the hatch for the boys to sleep and eat their lunches. Mary, with the features of a white girl was more or less smuggled into my cabin; sleeping on a leather couch and eating her School lunch.

Kind-hearted Captain Mac said, 'As long as the boys do not make a nuisance of themselves, they may stay on deck.'

These Indians, with no feeling of restriction when confronted with closed doors, went wherever they pleased. I had to keep our cabin door locked to prevent Mary from wandering into other cabins. Whenever I took her out on deck, I noticed two wealthy tourists, lounging in chairs, gazing through field glasses, peering down their noses at my little brood and me.

At four o'clock in the morning, the steward wakened me. I unglued my sleepy eyes, drew on clammy clothes, and made my way below to get Wilfred and Tommy ready to go ashore. I drew some comfort with the thought that on the morrow I could sleep in. All responsibility for Indians would roll off my shoulders. At five o'clock, the boys shinned down the ladder, jumped into their father's boat, and waved farewell.

Joe missed the other boys' company and asked if he could remain out on deck. It was such a lovely morning, I remained outside with him. We leaned over the deck rail and watched the morning break. That rosy glow, forerunner of the sun, crept slowly across the sky. The sun climbed higher and higher, and shed its warm rays all about us.

Joe's mind seemed to be drinking in the sky, the sea, and the gulls as they wheeled and banked about the vessel, then skimmed lightly over the water. More interested in the changing expressions on Joe's face than in gulls, I was trying to imagine what was passing through his mind. He broke the stillness by exclaiming, 'Whew, didn't he do that slick! Look, Nurse, at that gull perched on the rail. And did he swoop down on that floating garbage! See, there he goes with it in his bill!'

The gull soared upward with his rare tit-bit and balanced precariously on the rail. I thought, 'Gulls and Indians, how similar. Both forced to be scavengers.'

At seven o'clock, Joe's father brought his boat alongside the

167

Norah. Joe shinned down the rope, waved goodbye, and the last Indian boy vanished from my life. Mary had wakened, found herself alone in the cabin, and groped her way to the locked door. She must have felt like a captured bird. When I entered she threw her arms around me, and sobbed, 'Why did you lock me in here?' With the promise that soon she would be able to go out on deck and watch for her harbour, Alberni, I coaxed her back to bed.

At midday, the *Norah* docked at Alberni, and I took her to Mr Brant's secretary, who promised to keep an eye on her until he could decide how and where she would spend the night and the summer. The woman caring for her mother, and Aggie if she were still alive, had six other children to mind. Mary had dormant tuberculosis but had built up a resistance. With extra rest, cod liver oil and quantities of peanut butter at the School, she might live to grow up. It would be signing her death certificate to send her back to her own home.

At lunch an amusing incident made me smile and wonder if one year had made such a tremendous difference in my appearance and manners. One of the old dowagers, whom I had seen on deck, wrapped in her expensive, squirrel coat, dolled up to look like a spring chicken, gazed down her pince-nez, and enquired, 'Why did you leave your children at different places along the Coast? Are you sick and cannot care for them, or are you going for a vacation?'

I opened my mouth to explain, changed my mind, and replied, 'We all need a change and rest occasionally.' Then I suddenly realized I had changed, and had subconsciously adopted some of the Indians' stoicism – like Mr King.

That afternoon, out of harness, I felt ten years younger. A month's vacation loomed ahead of me. This would give me time to adjust myself before undertaking entirely new problems, with New Canadians in the West. I gave myself up to complete relaxation, and to meditate. After one year, would I still look like an Indian mother with five papooses? Would I still be free to enjoy nature's beauty? Would I be unemployed, or have to gaze longingly into shop windows?

I remained outside, watching the various moods of the waves. A huge wave broke in puff balls of white foam and flowed sinuously through a channel between squat towers of rock. The sun suddenly disappeared and heavy rain drops splashed on the water, making tiny shimmering whirlpools. The water beneath the overhanging cliffs loomed in the black abyss. It was almost impossible to conceive such a sudden change; danger, beauty, might, serenity, all blended into a fascinating picture. As I watched this mighty water, I wondered if many persons fully realized how much the Indians have contributed, especially as guides, in opening this western waterway to civilization. I also knew how few people appreciated this beautiful, coast scenery.

A sharp exclamation from another tourist, drew me back to earth. He exclaimed, 'Did you see how Captain Mac missed that protruding snag by a pinpoint?'

He snaked his course between a gravel bar, and manoeuvred the *Norah* past a shoal out into calm water. Just before we struck this dark water, the wave split and hissed under the stern, making the sudden calm more obvious.

The captain on the bridge shouted, 'Port.'

'Port,' repeated the steersman.

The *Norah* swung quickly seaward, just missing another huge, angry reef.

'Starboard a little,' shouted the captain.

'Steady!'

'Starboard,' shouted the captain, then, 'Half speed ahead.'

That day, more than on my first trip up this Coast, I realized how free the Indians must have felt, and how similar situations must have challenged them. I could actually see the primitive people, their paddles glistening, as with unwavering rhythm and unhampered strength, they paddled their canoes silently but swiftly, over the unexplored waters. I saw a people who had suffered unknown and untold hardships, today held in contempt by many of other races : a people with no war memorials, no band marching funerals, whose praises are seldom sung, a people who endured and enjoyed excrutiating cold, sickness, supple and active as the lynx, and had paddled through these rushing torrents. They had shot rapids, leaped rocks, and carried heavy burdens and canoes over long portages. A people who never mooched wearily up and down sidewalks, gazing

169

enviously into shop windows, but who wore a smile through storm, sunshine, famine, sickness and death. All the while their simple hearts looked to their Great Chief with awe and fear.

How noisy the train was as it rolled eastward. I could hear the words, 'Don't forget, don't forget . . .' which clicked on the great metal wheels.

The train sped on through the land where Indians, with their bows and arrows, had hunted deer and bear. Where young boys and old men, high up on the mountain side, unencumbered by worldly goods, had meditated on the wonders of their Great Spirit.

The hot air inside the coach was stifling, while cold drafts around the window raised prickly goose pimples. I burrowed deeper between the thick, tightly tucked bedding, and felt fenced in. Fagged, grimy, cold and cramped I wakened and snapped up the window blind and faced a new world. The first faint light of dawn was breaking. Birds balanced on wires. Snow capped mountains were left behind. The air was deliciously cool. Cows and horses cropped the grass ravenously. Curliques of blue smoke wafted upward from chimneys. I had a mental picture of the nomad Indians snuggled in buffalo robes. Safe from chilly, damp night, they slept under the stars and breathed the pure mountain air. Then, coming awake to just such a hushed, beautiful world, free to roam in unlimited space. How they must miss all the freedom and beauty shut away on reservations.

The train rushed down through hair pin curves and shot out of black, mysterious tunnels. Unable to tear myself away from the window, I gazed down on the giddy depth into the rocky canyon and rushing water. Mrs Baker, in the next seat, exclaimed, 'Do you think it is safe? All of us on the same side, looking over such a cliff. We . . . we . . will not upset, do you think? Isn't it beautiful, those rapids and misty spray, but it makes me dizzy! I would not pass over this route in the spring or fall. What if we should have a landslide?'

All that day, we watched the changing scenery. Tall trees and cliffs plummeted hundreds of feet above. Foaming streams far below and labouring train wheels under us. By craning our necks, we could get an ideal view of the eerie holes below, through which the engine would soon shoot, carrying us into Stygian blackness. Far, far above leaving black caves, the engine, with nervous jerks, angry mutterings, spells of shuddering, and unexpected piercing shrieks, puffed down, leaving heavy, rolling clouds of black smoke behind.

It took tons of dynamite to blast these tunnels, and the terrified Indians thought it was their angry Great Spirit belching fire from heaven on them.

We sped past stations with familiar historical names. I recalled how the early French and English reported that Indians were warriors worthy of the foe. In the 1914–18 World War more than four thousand joined the three services. Many of them were distinguished soldiers and won high rewards. How pioneers had welcomed their aid and guidance; learning the art of living in a new land.

The train sped eastward across the prairies. Gophers popped up beside holes in the sand, twitched their noses, tensed their ears, and vanished, leaving only a streak of yellow dust. In a moment they popped up a few feet away, their black eyes darting from side to side, whiskers quivering. Soon we left the prairies behind. The farther east the train carried us, the deeper and wider grew the line of demarcation between the atmosphere of reservation and white population life. Before I worked in the calm atmosphere of reservation life, I had never noticed the many unhappy faces and restless persons, such as I saw at station platforms and on trains, that were such a contrast with Indians' faces. The longer I thought over the matter the harder it was to realize that peace and happiness could ever be satisfactorily blended between Indians and people of other races, or at least for generations to come. One race possessing so much more worldly goods than it needed, living in beautiful homes, and enjoying expensive conveniences. Alongside, another race barely existing. My thoughts drifted back to so many persons I knew. They had all these luxuries, yet, unsettled and restless, they left their luxurious homes, whizzed through miles of barren country in order to live and enjoy a few hours, or a few days, near nature, the way Indians lived previously. Would this link – enjoyment of nature and its beauty – draw Indians and people of other races together? Indians and whites loved the Rocky Mountain scenery we had just left behind.

I came to the conclusion that assimilation of Indians with other races will depend on preserving the culture of Indians, combined with the best elements of other races. They need guidance from outside to encourage them to have a desire to help them see that it will benefit them to give up some of their undesirable customs and habits. But they must never be forced into a dull uniformity of customs of other people, like Tokawaka School children were. After all, Indians are human beings, not relics.

The further we left the West behind, the more I noticed the vast difference between the Indians' ideals and standards, and those of other races. And the more I seemed to be no longer myself, but another person returning to strange surroundings.

The train was passing through miles of burned-over waste and useless forest. Where Indians had taken the wealth of fish and animals from rapid streams and dense forests, men had slashed wantonly and destroyed huge timber, fish, and animals, then passed on. What Indians had left untouched for centuries had been robbed of its wealth overnight by carelessness. Where only a few years before thousands of Indians had been self-supporting, the train now rushed past falling-down buildings in ghost towns, barren, sandy land, denuded forests, and almost empty streams.

Strange how different a person's ideas can change in one year. Never before had I realised how deeply waste soil and sand storms, left in the wake of civilization, must have cut into Indians' hearts and how they must have felt when they heard of lives lost from rivers overflowing their banks, because men had taken the trees and soil that damned their natural courses.

From the train windows now, I saw everywhere advertisements screaming. 'Hot Dogs,' 'Potato Chips,' 'White Wash Laundry,' 'Black Horse Ale,' 'Craven A Cigarettes.' Beer bottles, glittering tin cans, soiled tissues, paper bags, and other junk littered the roadsides.

The white man had passed defiling beautiful scenery, polluting ponds, wasting and impoverishing the land. All of these articles will tell future excavators what type of civilization the North American continent supported in the 1900's.

All along the way, restaurants, placated the white man's presence, and distracted from the natural, beautiful scenery of the hills and valleys. Once a white man passes, it seems as though the landscape never remains the same.

I recalled how history stated that the Russian, Spanish, British, and French traders had vied with each other for supremacy in the fur and fish trade. As a result, the blood of many of the natives of North American Indians had slowly become adulterated through promiscuous relations with traders and sailors. These interlopers' licences often were unrestricted. Thus our School for full-blood Indians had children with Polynesian and Negroid features, Scandinavian complexions, and English and Scotch red heads. The full-blooded Indians previously looking to their chiefs for guidance, knew no class snobbery, there was equality among them. They accepted half and quarter breed children with the same attitude.

Arriving in my home town, I seemed to step suddenly from the unhurried, more or less harmonious life of the reservation, into the bickering family atmosphere. It was like stepping into another planet, filled with people constantly trying to insinuate themselves with materially great people. Everywhere I went, on the streets, in stores, and in homes, some people appeared to be trying to buy their way somewhere, or anywhere. They were rushing hither and yon in search of, but never finding that inner happiness enjoyed by those down-trodden Indians, whose ancestors once had a complex class system in their society, now living in squalor.

I felt small, lost and unimportant.

173

POSTSCRIPT

And so I left my peculiarly mature children – Freddie, with his ever-running nose and broad grin; Jeannie, with her winning smile and love of pretty things; orphaned John Mark, with his subtle and tactful way of getting things he wanted; Lucy, with her vanity; quiet, dreaming Peter, his mind full of Indian legends, or up in the clouds communing with his Great Spirit; silent, non-committal Philip; disgruntled Emma, sulking and longing to be free to marry and have children of her own; trustworthy, motherly Martha, watching over her charges; poor, pathetic Nixon, who would only have to suffer for a few years more.

Home among my own people, have they or I changed? Previously, I thought and lived as they did. Now they seem almost strangers. They seem to believe the whole wide earth revolves around their families and homes.

Everywhere I go now, I meet people agonising over trifles until I wonder how much longer it will be before civilized humanity will learn what Benjamin Franklin learned so many years ago, that contentment makes poor men rich, discontentment makes rich men poor.

It is my hope to encourage readers to take an interest in and read more about these natives of North America. Then and only then can one understand the many complex problems which confront Indians, the Department of Indian Affairs, religious organisations, and workers engaged by these institutions.

I thank God, who gave me the inspiration to train for a nurse. There is no other profession which gives greater compensation when day is done : the satisfaction after a miraculous recovery, or after ushering in a new life, or just helping the weary and sharing their troubles.

Florence Nightingale was right when she said that nursing is not a one-way traffic. The nurse soothes fevered brows and patients recover or not, but the nurse receives far more than she gives.

Now, as I write this book, there is the dawn of a new attitude to the problem. Perhaps the patience of the Indians will be rewarded at last, and their long awaited miracle in sight. At last, the people of Canada are gradually becoming aware of the vastness of the problem of these people in their midst. Progress is slow, but it is steady. The Church, the Department of Indian Affairs and the Board of Education have played an essential part in awakening in new generations of Indians a desire for integration. Much credit must also be given to the workers – perhaps even I played a small but significant part – who battle against the odds, and refused to succumb to difficulties. The viewpoint that I have so often heard expressed that 'the only good Indian is a dead one' must be a thing of the past.

Millions of dollars are being spent on education, and perhaps soon some return will be seen. The day school system is beginning to replace the residential system; and the children therefore have the benefits of both cultures. The Indian heritage is still too strong to be erased by foreign influences but perhaps bit by bit the best of both worlds will be combined. Suddenly Canadian Indians are getting almost as much attention as American Negroes; the national conscience has been awakened. A few outstanding Indians have important positions; the limelight is on them and they help to draw attention to the condition of the masses of their people.

Recently, the Indian Affairs Branch has acknowledged its past failure to cope with the problem and admits that reservations are without hope, and poverty stricken, and that its past policy has 'tend to emasculate development work at the community level.' It acknowledges the failure of the agent system, whereby the agent often becomes the only contact with the outside world for the reservation; that Indians who leave the reservations are worse off.

To remedy the situation crash courses have been given to 30 hand picked men, including several Indians who were then placed on key reservations with the object of teaching the Indians to raise their own standard of living to that of surrounding

communities. On this course one man said for the first time after
several years of working in white society he found himself 'at
home with the white man.' Their object was not to lead the
Indians, but to advise their chiefs to help the people. Another
plan is to pay grants into bank accounts for Indian councils,
and not to have funds administered by the agent. Trust was
the foundation on which to work, not coercion to adopt white
methods.

So perhaps at last the first faltering steps have been taken
towards the policy of self-growth, of leaving the Indian to walk
towards integration by his own steps, and not to be dragged
along with leading reins. People who are really interested in the
problem have been sent to help the Indians, and not as
previously just anybody who applied for a job as a source of
comparatively easy living well away from effective government
control. The corruption and negligence so often found when I
was working among them are being replaced by mediators to
interpret the Indian viewpoint to Ottawa.

But success is still far in the future. The first steps have been
taken, but meanwhile the suffering, the slums and the general
poverty continue. 'The white man has taken away the things
of the Indian,' was the cry. Slowly pioneers are replacing them,
but it is very slow and meanwhile the Indians remain, as the
Indian Affairs branch admits, 'bystanders on the national scene.'